AS OTHERS SEE US

As Others See Us

A Conversation on Cultural Differences

Divya Jhingran
S.N. Balagangadhara

First Published 2015

Revised 2019

© Divya Jhingran, 2015

Title ID: 5296199

ISBN-13: 978-1507832332

O wad some Pow'r the giftie gie us
To see oursels as ithers see us!
ROBERT BURNS, 1786

CONTENTS

Acknowledgements

ACKNOWLEDGEMENTS

This book is based on actual conversations with Prof. S. N. Balagangadhara. These conversations took place over a number of years, included many participants, and covered many topics. In addition, the ideas for this book were drawn from the following articles and books: Balagangadhara, S.N. (1985) *We Shall Not Cease From Exploration*; Balagangadhara, S.N. (2012) *Reconceptualizing India Studies*, Delhi: Oxford University Press; Balagangadhara, S.N., Jhingran, Divya (2014) *Do All Roads Lead To Jerusalem? The Making of Indian Religions*, Delhi: Manohar; Balagangadhara S.N. (2006) *Some Theses on Colonial Consciousness;* Balagangadhara, S.N. (2005) *How to Speak for the Indian Traditions, An Agenda For The Future;* Balagangadhara, S.N. *Comparative Anthropology and Action Sciences: An Essay on Knowing to Act and Acting to Know;* Claerhout, Sarah (2010)*'Losing My Tradition': Conversion, Secularism and Religious Freedom in India*, Unpublished PhD Dissertation; De Roover, Jakob (forthcoming) *Europe, India, and the Limits of Secularism* (Delhi: Oxford University Press).

CHAPTER I

THE PHALLUS AND OTHER FALLACIES

Reeti: Once again I'm flummoxed after a conversation I just had with someone in my yoga class. I met this American woman who's interested in learning about Hinduism, and today she asked me if I believed in Shiva. Quite frankly, I had no idea how to respond. To me, it's absurd to say yes, but at the same time, it doesn't sound right to say no either. After all, I do love chanting on *Shiva Ratri*, and I kept a fast for Shiva every Monday for several years. It's funny that I cannot answer a simple question like this without feeling like no matter what I say, it somehow sounds wrong.

Arya: I often find myself in a similar predicament. Some of the questions that sound perfectly normal when Americans ask them, cannot be expressed the same way in any Indian language. It's frustrating that although I can sense that there's something's wrong with the question, it's hard to articulate what the problem is exactly. That's why I'm so thrilled to be together for a few days with Leela who can help us unravel precisely these sorts of problems.

Leela: I'm glad to be here too. As you know, I've spent the last couple of decades reflecting on these matters and on developing my ideas about cultural differences. If I had to put it in a nutshell, I would say that as far as the Indian traditions are concerned, there is something fundamentally wrong with the way in which they are described. Most of what we have learnt about ourselves is what has been said about us by western culture. We relate to our own culture the way the West has understood it and taught us to understand it. Since this doesn't gel with our actual experience, we end up at a loss to explain our own traditions.

Arya: This sounds absurd. I agree I have a problem, but I always thought that this is because I did not have a very traditional upbringing.

Leela: Believe me the problem goes deeper than that. I can give you a few examples right off the bat to illustrate what I mean. Most of us learnt English through the mediation of our local languages. However, it's not as if we established the equivalence of certain words because we knew what they meant; rather we were merely taught that these are the equivalents of certain words in our languages. We learnt, for instance, that *puja* means 'worship', *deva* means 'god', *tapas* means 'penance', and *murti* means 'idol'. Such translations work at a superficial level and most of us get by with them. But when we run up against problems, we are unable to articulate what is wrong with these depictions and why they don't really reflect our experience. Are we really phallus worshippers or cow worshippers? If not, then what exactly are we doing? We have no way of answering such questions. This is because we no longer have access to our own traditions in any direct fashion. At the same time, we don't have an understanding of western culture either. Our only way out of this predicament is to begin with a study of western culture and to better understand western culture.

Reeti: But we're here to understand Indian culture not western culture! Of course I'm interested in understanding all cultures, but right now I thought the problems we were trying to solve had to do with our inability to articulate how we really think about the Indian traditions. If translation poses a problem, let's just use our own words and be done with it.

Leela: I'm afraid we're way too deep in the rut to come out of it so easily. You see, we've inherited a certain way of thinking that's been in place for the past 300 years. The dominant conceptual schemes that we use in thinking about many things have emerged from western culture and were formulated in European languages. We inevitably take recourse to such conceptual schemes *even when we speak in our own languages*.

Reeti: That may be. But it still feels like a waste of time to get sidetracked into these tangential matters.

Leela: I'm afraid this is the crux of the matter. The British came up with many descriptions of Indian culture and its so-called religions. These descriptions reflected a pattern in the experience of the British. If you accept that Hinduism and Buddhism refer to religions in Indian culture, this means that you accept that the patterns in western cultural experience are true descriptions of the structures that exist in India. They are not. They are a reflection of western culture. In any case, the more disconcerting thing is that Indians have accepted this way of looking at the world as if it is the only way of looking at the world. The days of colonization may be long gone, but in their wake they have left behind a colonial consciousness that acts as a distorting lens that prevents us from viewing things in any other way except in the terms described by the West.

Arya: I understand that some people complain about how our religions are "European constructs", but I think it is a matter of practical convenience to just refer to them as religions now. In any case, why is it necessarily the case that the British experience of India and our own experience of India must be different?

Leela: When we make observations about societies and cultures, what we observe differs from observer to observer. If you will grant that there are cultural differences between the East and the West, then you must grant that people from these cultures experience the social and cultural world differently. Many experiences are entirely culture-specific. At the time of our colonization, this raised problems because the experience of the colonizers was often not the same as that of the colonized natives. Our colonizers described our culture in the only way they knew how – the way *they* experienced it. Now that we have come to accept their descriptions, we are forced to distort our own experience to make it rhyme with these descriptions. In this way we are denied access to our own experience.

Arya: Don't we experience things at a human level too, not just at a cultural level? We may worship different gods, but it is still worship. What difference does it make whether you kneel before a statue of Mary or that of Ganesha? I don't think it is so off the mark to say that, at a human level, people from different cultures experience the same phenomenon, even if the framework they use to describe their experience is not the same.

Leela: I don't agree at all. When you use a word like 'worship', you are using a concept that describes a culture-specific experiential pattern that is based on western Christianity. You cannot use the same word to refer to another completely different culture-specific experiential pattern without misrepresenting the case.

Perhaps an analogy will help illustrate the nature of the problem. This is an example used by Norwood Hanson, a prominent thinker in the philosophy of science. Suppose you walk into a laboratory and see a scientist busy at work. You see all the apparatus crowded on the table, small cups filled with something luminous, spools of wire, metal pins, mirrors, and batteries. You see the scientist fiddle with the wires, you see a flash of light and some of the metal pins start jumping up and down. Fascinated, you ask him if he's trying to make the metal pins jump around, and he responds: "No, I'm actually measuring the electric resistance of the spools." Now, do you and the scientist observe the same phenomena? You do not – even if you are in the same room and looking at the same thing. In much the same way, both our western theorists and a local Indian see the same social or cultural world, but they observe a different pattern. Here it is misleading to say that people from different cultures experience the same phenomena. It could well be that some people experience seeing someone kneel before a statue of Ganesha as a form of devil worship.

Arya: Now, let's not get carried away. The analogy certainly helps, but it would be better if you narrowed it down with some more concrete examples.

Leela: Well, the starkest, most overarching example, as I already mentioned, has to do with the way in which the Indian traditions have been re-cast in terms of religion. Bear in mind that the earliest travelers to India had not reported seeing any religion in India. Both the Chinese and the Greek travelers described what they saw not in terms of religion but in terms familiar to them from their own traditions. It was the Muslims first and later the Europeans who characterized Indian culture in terms of religions. Now by adopting their descriptions of Indian society we actually understand it less and less.

What if there is another way of looking at Indian culture? One that more accurately describes India and her traditions *without referring to religion at all*, and one that is richer and more satisfying? We are unable to access this alternative way of seeing things because of the current framework we're trapped in. Sooner or later this richness will be completely lost to us. This is why I believe it is important to question the line of continuity between the western descriptions of India and our own. This is the only way we will be able to break out of the colonial patterns of experience.

Reeti: I have to admit that I often feel a sort of dissonance when I read about how our culture is depicted not just by the West but also by Indians. The funny thing is that everything feels quite normal when I do my *puja*, or participate in any of the other practices or holidays. But seeing the same acts described in the literature somehow does not ring true. In fact, the portrayals often come across as absurd.

Leela: I think this is a challenge for most of us. This is ironic because if there's one thing that our traditions have emphasized, it is to reflect upon experience. Now the most troubling thing that we have on our hands is the problematic nature of contemporary Indian experience itself – or rather our inability to access it.

Arya: What do you mean we cannot access our own experience?

Leela: Let me see how I can explain this. As is the case with most Indians, I too learnt English through an Indian language. I learnt too that unlike our 'gods' the Judeo-Christian God was spelled with a 'big G' as we used to say at the time. It was not exactly clear to me what this God was. I just assumed that 'God' referred to the entity you chose, since in our culture we tend to choose our favorite *deva*. Mine, for instance was Shiva. Somehow, I fell in love with this madcap ascetic with his abode in the cremation grounds, his tendency to be easily provoked to anger, his garland of snakes and the whole aura about him. One day, I must have been around fourteen, I 'discovered' that *linga* meant phallus (a penis as it was explained to me), and that it was a symbol of male fertility. This meant that when we went to do *puja* in our nearby temple, we actually went to worship a male penis. I was terribly confused and embarrassed by this explanation. I felt that it was wrong, but I did not know what to say to justify my feeling. My protests merely generated mockery from the person who had broken this news to me: "How many have you seen?" they jeered. But my sense of wrongness never left me. This, then, is one of the earliest incidents in my life that I can recall relating to the distortion of my experience with respect to our traditions.

Arya: I can understand that. But you quite clearly knew that you were confused and embarrassed. Why, then, do you refer to this as an inability to access your experience?

Leela: Perhaps this other story of a friend of mine will help illustrate my point better. As you no doubt know, it is a common practice in India for male friends to walk around holding hands, or with their arms slung across each other's shoulders. In India there's no significance attached to these gestures other than that of being close friends. Well, this friend of mine embarks on his first ever trip to Europe and what does he see there? Men, not just holding hands, but openly embracing and kissing! Now, although he knew about homosexuality in the abstract, he had never seen any of the outward expressions of gay affection or sexuality. This was a rather novel and fascinating discovery for him, in Amsterdam, I believe it was. Anyway, he comes back to India and meets up with his old buddies – the very same ones with whom he would walk around arm in arm with all the time. But somehow, he could no longer hold hands with them or allow them to sling their arms across his shoulder. Such acts had taken on a whole new meaning. Even though he had no problem doing the same before he went to Europe, after his return he could not. It was embarrassing; but he could not share this feeling with his friends who had never been to Europe. Nor could he tell them to stop doing it because it would have seemed rude and incomprehensible to them.

Arya: So you're saying that your friend's exposure to the big wide world changed his perspective? This happens to all of us sooner or later. I'm not sure how this relates to what we are discussing.

Leela: The point I'm trying to make is that his original experience was no longer available to him. It was overwritten by his new experience. This, in a way, is what has been going on in India and in many other parts of the world for the past 300 years. We have learned to talk in a way that is so alien to our culture that the original experience is no longer accessible to us. Now, a quarter of a century later, I have come to realize the importance of developing the conceptual tools needed to interrogate these experiences. Not mine alone but those of an entire culture. Now I am able to understand the significance of the feeling of embarrassment I felt on being told that the *Shivalinga* is a phallus.

Reeti: To be honest, I have never been able to relate to the idea that the *Shivalinga* is a phallus. I too discovered this sometime in my teens. I remember telling this to my mother, who, of course, told me that I was talking nonsense. Being the teenager that I was, I took this to be just another example of my mother's cluelessness. But now that I think about it, it does not seem plausible that people who do daily *puja* to Shiva would not know that the *Shivalinga* symbolized a phallus if that was something worth knowing about. This is the sort of thing we learn from textbooks generated by the West and I agree that there is a huge disconnect between what is described in the textbooks and the attitude of the average Hindu.

Leela: The problem is that these descriptions trivialize and distort our experiences. When I learned that we were merely worshipping the male penis it made me feel doubly foolish. First, because I was worshipping the penis; and second, because I did not even know that I was worshipping the penis. Of course, the point of this discussion is not to question the moral right of the British or Americans or anyone else to speak in the name of our communities, but whether such speech constitutes knowledge of any kind.

Reeti: I think I'm beginning to see the significance of what you're saying. Even though most Hindus continue their practices like they have always done, our way of talking about our traditions has undergone a huge change. This must be the line of continuity between the British descriptions and our own descriptions of the Indian traditions that you are referring to.

Leela: This is but one small example just to set the ball rolling. Western scholarship on the Indian traditions makes many of us squirm. With their profound fetish for symbolism, they read all kinds of meanings into our *puja* of the *Shivalinga* and other things. To them, it is not a *puja* of Shiva at all but a subconscious acknowledgement of some repressed notion of fertility, or whatever else takes their fancy.

Arya: Hang on a second! I'm all for symbolic interpretations and don't see why you are so dismissive of them. Why can't the *lingam* be interpreted as a symbol for the phallus even if most Indians do not see the symbolism?

Leela: But that's exactly the point! If this is not how we see it, why accept this depiction? Why can't we look at it the more straightforward way, like we've done for thousands of years? The *lingam* is not a symbol of anything or anybody. The *lingam* is how Shiva's *puja* is done, as against, say, how we do *puja* to Vishnu. Please note that I am merely being descriptive and am not providing any interpretation, whereas you are agreeable about doing precisely that. Why do you believe that our ancestors took to doing *puja* to a symbol instead of simply saying that they do *puja* to the penis, irrespective of whose penis it is? It could not be because they were prudish or repressed. If women went about bare-breasted, and we gave the world the *Kama Sutra*, and built explicitly sexual temples, surely our ancestors would not have been inhibited about saying that they worshipped a penis? Why did they have to invent symbolism for the penis, deny that it was merely a penis and cook up the utterly fantastic story that it was the *Shivalinga*? Well, my dear, you need to make this plausible to me. Why this devious route and not a direct declaration that they worship a penis? Until you come up with a satisfactory story, I think I am justified in insisting that we do what our ancestors did. We do *puja* to Shiva in the form of the *lingam*.

Arya: But if you consider all of the folklore, it seems quite clear that the *Shivalinga* is the phallus of Shiva.

Leela: If that was really the case most Hindus would not have to learn about it from western scholars. Unlike the Bible, the *Puranas* (epics) do not have to be true, or believed to be true, for them to play the role that they do in Indian culture. The presuppositions of your question, although common ones in western scholarship, are based on an ignorance about the genre of 'myth' and the role it plays in India. The British took bits and pieces culled from Indian folklore and reproduced it in textbooks as an 'explanation' about Indian culture. It's important to understand that stories are *not* explanations. They're not meant to be factual descriptions of the world, nor do they describe factual events. They do not claim to be doing that either.

Reeti: Let me see if I can pinpoint where the problem lies. We do not describe Christians as performing crucifix-worship, so perhaps by the same token we cannot describe *puja* to the *Shivalinga* as phallus worship. Is that the underlying problem with this depiction?

Leela: Not really. Idol worship is strictly forbidden in Christianity and Christians would feel insulted if they were to be described as crucifix-worshippers. Nevertheless, they would at least be able to relate to the words 'crucifix' and 'worship'. The problem in our case is not the same. There is an important cognitive point lurking underneath this so let me see if I can highlight it with an example. Say, in the context of physics, would you say that the word 'mass' refers to something that is a variable or something that is invariant?

Arya: Well, a Newtonian would say 'invariant'; an Einsteinian would say 'variable'.

Leela: Right. So the point is that our decision about which description represents the truth has nothing to do with the meaning of a word but depends, instead, on our background theories. Only by considering what the criteria are for choosing between the two competing theories can we decide what the words mean. What often appears to be a dispute about the meanings of words is actually a dispute about a theory or a theology.

Bearing this in mind, now consider whether, in the context of *puja*, *Shivalinga* refers to anything other than Shiva. The short answer is no. We are, therefore, compelled to grant the only possible conclusion: *Shivalinga* is the form in which we do *puja* to Shiva. This mind-numbing conceptual tour merely tells us what our grandmothers had told us all along, in all their simplicity.

Reeti: Sadly this doesn't resolve the larger problem. How do we choose between competing ways of looking at things? There's a whole slew of western scholarship that seems to be gaining more and more ground. Who sets the terms of the debate?

Leela: We need to reflect on our experience and say what we really see, not what we've learned to say. After years of reflection, I am finally in a place where I am able to articulate my objections to these nonsensical depictions. Let's say an American Indologist comes along and asserts that "when you worship the *lingam*, you worship a phallus". You can either accept this interpretation or reflect on your experience. Most likely you will conclude that when you go into a Shiva temple, you do not go there to worship a phallus; you merely go there to do *puja* to Shiva.

Reeti: Is that all? Can we rest with the idea that the West has its way of looking at things and we have another? This is not satisfying enough for me.

Leela: Well then, in that case you can always give them a strong dose of their own theology. You see, the English word 'worship' basically comes from Christian theology. According to this theology, you can either worship God or the Devil and nothing else. Under no interpretation of such a theology could one consider Shiva to be God, leaving us with only one possibility that Shiva is the devil. If this is what they want to say – that we are worshipping the devil – in that case, the discussion is not about a translation issue but rather is a discussion of Christian theology. That is why, you see, these are not linguistic issues; they are theoretical issues.

We have taken on the western way of talking without understanding what we are talking about. The greatest failing of Indians in this regard has been a complete lack of interest in trying to understand Christianity. In this religion, what worship is, how one worships, and in what form one worships cannot be decided by mere mortals but is something that requires revelation from God. This revelation not only tells us that there is only one God, but also that there is a false God, that is to say, the Devil. If you worship anything other than the one true God, it means that you are worshipping the Devil. The road to salvation (please, do not confuse this with *moksha* or *nirvana*) lies in worshipping the true God.

Reeti: But how are they supposed to figure out who the true God is if they cannot just choose their god and what does worship mean to them?

Leela: We know who the true God is because he has revealed himself (again, please do not confuse this with *avatars*). This revelation is contained in the Bible which is why the Bible is referred to as the word of God. In the Bible, God also specifies how we ought to worship him. He has commanded us not to create idols. This should make it clear why you can practically rewrite the history of Christianity and Islam based on their hatred of idol worship. So you need to take this very seriously and try to understand the implications of translating *puja* as worship and *murti* as idol. You can only worship the true God and not his image. Any other worship is devil worship. If you insist on translating *puja* as worship then the implication is that you are doing devil worship.

Reeti: I think I see a glimmer of recognition in what you just said. Recently I participated in a community program that was held at the local church of our township in Maryland. A variety of people were invited to talk about their diverse faiths. While we were walking down the hall, the organizer whispered to our speaker not to use the word 'idol' at all since that would make some people in the congregation very uncomfortable. I was a bit taken aback by this. Of course I knew that idol worship is considered bad, but it had never occurred to me how much of a bad thing it was considered to be. But quite aside from this, our own traditions too criticize idol worship at times. Is there something intrinsically wrong with it?

Leela: It is true that our traditions do criticize *murtis*, gods, gurus, and advise us to kill our Buddhas and so on. But this has nothing to do with idol worship, devil worship, or false gods. Those statements are made in a whole other context, under a whole other theoretical framework.

Arya: Frankly, the implications you point out seem purely academic and I feel like our contemporary way of talking is a practical and harmless way of describing our traditions.

Leela: Of course we've always been the quintessential blind heathens who believe that Christians experience Christianity the way Hindus experience their traditions. There's no arguing with that. The problem, if I must repeat it a hundred times, does not lie in our lack of understanding of the English language but in our lack of understanding of western culture which has been shaped by Christianity. We have no clue about the extent to which Christian theology has made a home for itself in the linguistic practice of Indian culture. Without making an effort to study the West we will continue to look at the Semitic religions as human expressions and human creations. From within our framework, we cannot even begin to understand what they say about themselves, that is, that they are not human creations but the revelations of God. Being of human creation, in the context of their religions, amounts to being the work of the devil.

Reeti: This seems a bit contorted no matter how many times you repeat it. I still find it hard to accept that in order to understand my own culture, I'm expected to first understand Christianity. All I can agree on is that I feel a sense of wrongness somewhere but I cannot seem to pinpoint the nature of this wrongness.

Leela: As you know, I've spent a great deal of time thinking about this. Colonization was not just about occupying lands and extracting revenues. It goes deeper than that. It is about denying the colonized peoples and cultures their own experience; of making them aliens to themselves; of actively preventing any description of their own experience, except in terms defined by the colonizers.

Arya: But isn't this alienation that we experience no different from what any believer undergoes in the West, when they discover that God is dead? Are our travails anything other than a simple story of modernity as it plays out in India?

Leela: It cannot possibly be the same thing. There is too vast a cultural difference between the Indian pagan world and the religious world of the West to even remotely have the same experience in this regard. Discovering that a *lingam* is a penis does not rob me of my world the same way atheism robs a believer of their world in western culture. There are so many reasons why these two processes are not even remotely similar.

Arya: I don't think I understand. Can you elaborate on this?

Leela: There's a nice story in the *Chandogya Upanishad* that
will help illustrate this: It appears that one day Prajapati
declared: He who has found the Self (*Atman*) and understands it, obtains all desires. The *devas* and the *asuras*
both heard these words, and said: Well, let us search for
that Self, by finding which, all desires will be ours.
Thus, Indra from the *devas* and Virochana from the
asuras, each without communicating with the other, approached Prajapati. They dwelt there as pupils for thirty-
two years. Then Prajapati asked them: "For what purpose have you both dwelt here?" They both replied: "A
saying of yours has been going around, oft-repeated...we have both dwelt here because we wish for
that Self." Prajapati makes them both look in a pan of
water and asks them what they see. They say they see
the reflection of their own bodies. He makes them dress
up nicely and look again into the pan of water and asks
them what they see. They say: "Just as we are, well
adorned, with our best clothes and clean, thus we are
both there, Sir, well adorned, with our best clothes and
clean." Prajapati said: "This is the Self, this is the im-
mortal, the fearless...this is Brahman". They both went
away, satisfied in their hearts.

Prajapati reflects on their absence of critical thought and
thinks that whichever of the two follows this line of
thinking will perish. The story continues: "Now Virochana, satisfied in his heart, went to the *asuras* and
preached that doctrine to them, that the self (the body)
alone is to be worshipped, that the self (the body) alone
is to be served, and that he who worships the self and
serves the self, gains both worlds, this and the next."

The story further continues about what Indra did, but
that is not relevant right now. One of the most obvious
points in the story is that the *asuras* and *devas* both seek
enlightenment! Quite obviously, as this story makes
clear, enlightenment does not involve believing in some

deva for the simple reason that the *devas* too thirst after enlightenment. Moreover, to reach this state, as it becomes evident when we follow the story further, no grace of any kind of 'God' is particularly necessary. What is required is the need to think through. From this it follows that enlightenment can be the result of one's own effort. It is a deserved reward that is in proportion to the effort you put in. Virochana's insight that the body requires worshipping because it is the 'Self' is a wrong answer because it is superficial. The answer, however, is not false. As the story evolves further, the reader appreciates that the *asura's* answer is superficial because Indra provides a deeper answer. But any answer is superficial only relative to a deeper one. That does not make Virochana's answer false or one that would bring his world crashing down. Virochana's insight appears materialistic or 'atheistic'; yet, the story seems to condone it as a *possible* answer, even if superficial.

The discovery that all there is to life is the life one has, or the body one has, does not rob an Indian of anything. To put it sharply, in the Indian traditions, atheism of a particular sort can also be a way of reaching enlightenment. This claim is not even remotely similar to the shock of discovering in western culture that 'God is dead'. The Indian traditions are not dependent on God the way Judaism, Christianity and Islam are.

Arya: I guess this goes back to what you said earlier – if we use religious vocabulary, we invariably end up with some or the other variant of Christian theology, even if it's atheism we talk about. But don't you think that this is merely our problem, I mean specifically us, the English-educated Indians, who are partly westernized and thus are that much more out of touch with our own traditions?

Leela: Not at all. In fact, if you go down that route, you will be logically compelled to say that there is some such thing as an 'authentic' Indian or an 'authentic' Hindu experience. That simply cannot be the case. Are we supposed to go deep in the deserts of Rajasthan or high on some Himalayan mountaintop to find the authentic Indian? My questions are about twenty-first century India and its present culture, which has absorbed and adapted many things from other cultures in many different ways. It is this set of Indian traditions that interests me. What does it mean to say that we are not authentically Indian or quasi-westernized? In fact, the greatest strength of our culture lies in the fact that this is a non-question as far as the Indian traditions are concerned.

Outside of Bangalore, there lives a well-known swami with an ashram. People from different parts of India come to have his *darshan* almost every day. Most people don't know his name, and he is simply called the 'Belgian Swamiji'. He came from Belgium to India more than two decades ago, and eventually set up an ashram there. The Indians who come to visit him do not consider him any less of a swami because he is Belgian. It does not make any sense, in such a context, to ask questions like who is the authentic Hindu. Me, you, or the Belgian swami? We all are that, both to ourselves as well as to others. We must not sacrifice this strength of our traditions when we challenge people from other cultures about the things they say and the tracts they produce. The objection is not that the West has theorized about Indians but the fact that what they have said happens to be rubbish.

Arya: If it's any consolation, we're not the only ones who have been singled out in this regard. Western descriptions of all other cultures have a tendency to distort and trivialize. I don't think the Africans or the Native Americans are too happy about how their cultures have been depicted.

Leela: Of course they aren't. The early European travelers carried their cultural framework everywhere they went and produced the same results.

Are you familiar with James Frazer's book *The Golden Bough*? This is an anthropological collection of stories full of explanations about practices in different cultures. The Austrian philosopher, Ludwig Wittgenstein, wrote some deeply insightful critical *Remarks* after reading Frazer's book. He thought that Frazer's descriptions transformed all non-western cultures into ridiculous ones. A case in point is Frazer's discussion of the Native American rain dance. If you were to ask the 'Rain Doctor' why his people dance for the rain, in all probability you'd get to hear a story. Now, when western anthropologists began to weigh in on this, they described it as an *explanation* about the performance of the rain dance. Assume for a moment that this is indeed the case. The conclusion you will be compelled to draw is that the members of this group are a bunch of fools. Do they really believe that their jumping up and down is the cause of the rains? Frazer tries to explain the practice of rain dancing by attributing a set of beliefs to the people. The attribution of such beliefs, says Wittgenstein, 'explains' human practices only by trivializing them. He calls such an attempt at providing explanations a "sickness". He also wonders why the rain dance is performed only during the rainy season. Perhaps we would do well to think Wittgenstein's question through.

Reeti: Perhaps they were just channeling their spiritual energy to pray for water for their crops?

Leela: Of course one can come up with any number of *ad hoc* explanations, as if some people believe that their prancing around in the fields will cause the rains to come. So if the natives are taught about irrigation, they will become rational and scientific and begin to understand the superstitious nature of their practices and stop dancing?

Wittgenstein draws attention to the absurdity of this argument. The Rain Doctor knows about irrigation and says that this has nothing to do with the rain dance. There is no need to explain the rain dance by speaking about the need for irrigation or anything else.

It is important to note that Wittgenstein is not arguing that some practice in a culture is beyond analysis or criticism just because it is a practice in that culture. He is saying something like this: do not confuse a distorted description of a practice with its explanation.

Reeti: I might add that in today's politically correct climate, people tend to justify cultural practices one way or another, either symbolically or otherwise, but in that case they merely end up sounding condescending.

Leela: That's very true. It's not as if there are no outrageous practices in human cultures. The point is that no cultural practice that has been transmitted through successive generations should be explained by attributing beliefs to its practitioners in such a way that the beliefs make the practitioners come out stupid. As Wittgenstein put it, "it will never be plausible to say that mankind does all that out of sheer stupidity." Wittgenstein remarked that all Frazer does is to make the practices plausible to people who think as he does. Now, what I have been pondering about for the last couple of decades is this: Wittgenstein was probably not just thinking about individuals. In fact, what Frazer did was the dominant way of doing in *the West*. We could paraphrase Wittgenstein's remark thus: All that Frazer does is to make the practices plausible to people in the West.

Arya: I'm not sure I get the significance of what you mean.

Leela: This is what Wittgenstein's insight boils down to: To make sense of practices, people in the West search for beliefs. They think that practices are an expression of beliefs. However, as far as the Rain Doctor is concerned, he is simply following his tradition. It is about what his people do, and not what his people believe. Trying to explain a practice by referring to a theory or a belief is *the only way* for the West to make sense of others. The cultural constraints on the western intellect are such that they are unable to see that actions can derive their consistency from actions themselves. In the western world, for some action to be coherent, a belief, a theory, or a worldview is needed which lends coherence to actions. This fixation on tying practices to beliefs, this "sickness" of western culture, is what we Hindus have been infected with. The problem I would now like to solve is why we succumbed to this as if this western belief-oriented way is the only way to look at things.

Arya: Whew, you just opened up a whole new can of worms. The mind boggles and lunch beckons. I think we all need a long siesta to fortify ourselves for the next phase of the discussion.

CHAPTER II

WHAT COMES FIRST, A THEORY
OR A FACT?

Arya: I've been mulling over our discussion, and the more I think about it, the more doubts I have. I think that, in general, all human beings tend to be belief-driven, so it seems wrong to suggest that Indians have adopted this way of talking from the West.

Leela: Of course human beings hold all sorts of beliefs. What I am questioning is the idea that human practices are based on beliefs. This idea is grounded in Christian theology where reason plays a central role. This way of thinking is quite alien to our traditions.

Arya: But long before Christianity, the Greeks and Romans also provided a rational foundation for their practices. So it cannot be something that arose solely as a result of Christianity. It must be something that Christians share with pagan cultures.

Leela: Reason was important in pagan thought only to the extent that it was a guide to human action, restrained human practices, or curbed superstition. But it was not a *foundation for beliefs*. If you're not so easily convinced, I can take you on a brief detour into Antiquity to retrace the history of this idea and show how it ties in to Christianity.

Arya: Sure, I'd be up for that.

Leela: The Greeks and Romans, as you know, had a number of gods and goddesses. Alongside these various deities, they also had numerous philosophical schools that often disputed about whether the gods were real or not. However, their religious practice was not dependent upon the status of the gods as being real or unreal. For example, thinkers such as Cicero and Plutarch who debated whether the gods were real, or even worth venerating, nevertheless officiated as priests and were meticulous about fulfilling their religious obligations.

Even though the word 'religion' comes from the Latin *'religio'*, the nature of the Roman *religio* seems to have been something completely different from what goes by the word 'religion' today. To the Romans, the 'truth' of their religion did not depend on the proof for or against the existence of the gods, but instead had to do with the antiquity of their practices. Their *religio* was a set of ancestral practices which they continued because of the authority they granted to the wisdom of their forefathers. Their *religio* must be understood more in terms of what we understand by the word 'tradition' these days. Basically, philosophical discourse about truth or belief was irrelevant to traditional practices which were retained merely because they were handed down from generation to generation.

Arya: If that was indeed the case, then why were there religious clashes? I mean, if, like you say, beliefs did not matter, then how are we to make sense of the persecution of the Jews and Christians by the Romans?

Leela: In this context, the fundamental objection that the Romans had was that these religions refused to recognize the traditions of other peoples and places as valid. The Jews claimed that their ancestral practice forbade them from worshipping the various Roman deities. The Christians could not follow the route taken by the Jews because of the simple fact that they were a people without a tradition, and, as such, they were accused of atheism by the Romans. Remember, in the Roman milieu, *religio* was akin to tradition. The Christians had to show that Christianity was a religion even though it was no tradition. They met this challenge by arguing that they were the followers of true beliefs and therefore their religion was true. By opposing their *beliefs* to Roman *practices*, the Christians brought about a fundamental shift. Religion, which so far had been almost synonymous with tradition, was now countered to tradition. The Christians claimed that through Jesus Christ they had rediscovered the true religion which had been present in man from the time of creation but had gotten lost because devil worship had taken over. Therefore, Christianity was not only much older than all other traditions but it was the only true doctrine. So you see, right from its inception Christianity had to rely on beliefs and the *truth* of these beliefs.

Reeti: But how can following a belief be equivalent to following a tradition, since there isn't a clear correlation between beliefs and practices?

Leela: This is because the Christians claimed that their practices expressed their teachings. If the teachings they accept are true, it follows that their practices are likewise true. Thus was formed a link between belief and practice that never existed before. By creating this link, Christianity reduced the Roman traditions to 'religion' as we understand the term today. These were now regarded as a variant of religion, and paganism, as the Christians claimed, was nothing but an expression of false or corrupt beliefs. Fast forward through the centuries and it brings us to our current understanding of religion, as developed by the Christians, which tells us that religion is something based on beliefs, doctrines, and so on and so forth. It is through this lens that the western world looks at *all* other cultures, and it is this stance that we too have adopted. This is one of the most fundamental manifestations of our colonial consciousness.

Reeti: This is all rather fascinating but I won't go so far as to say that all of us have internalized this way of thinking.

Most Hindus will readily agree that Hinduism is not really a religion but is more of a way of life.

Leela: Do you realize that sitting on your couch and watching football all day long is also a way of life? Almost anything can be called a way of life. This is the most meaningless statement, if ever there was one. In fact, every religion is a way of life, so it doesn't help to make this claim as a way of distinguishing Hinduism from religion.

Reeti: Okay, point taken. But whether you call it a religion or anything else, does not change anything much for most people. We are free to celebrate our festivals, do our *pujas*, chant our scriptures, and practice our traditions in our own way. A rose by any other name smells just as sweet, as they say. In the larger scheme of things, I don't think it matters.

Leela: But it does matter. We've come to a point where the pluralism of Indian culture is losing its vibrancy and where a mutual lack of understanding among the 'heathens' and the religious is leading to horrible tragedies. This is happening partly because the Indian intellectuals have adopted a western understanding of their own cultural traditions and see them as religions. Because of this, these thinkers are confronted with a dilemma: either they become proponents of western secularism or they become advocates of aggressive movements which try to defend the indigenous 'religions' of India. You can see this play out all the time with the Indian secularists pitted against the Hindu fundamentalists. I am convinced that there is a way out of this dilemma. A better understanding of the Indian traditions will show us that we have our own resources to safeguard pluralism and that these are much more effective than the bogus idea of secularism. A new way of looking at the Indian traditions is necessary as an alternative to the colonial depiction of looking at them as religions. And more broadly speaking, a new way of looking at western culture is equally necessary.

Arya: I'm not even sure what I'm supposed to understand by 'the West'. In this age of globalization, it seems almost arbitrary to pinpoint something as being typical of the West. This may have been true up until the last century, but does not seem so relevant now.

Leela: The 'West' must be understood as a cultural term and not a geographical one. From a twenty-first century perspective, the West is no longer the pagan West of Greece and Rome. There has been such a radical transformation of pagan ideas that these would not be recognizable to the pagans of antiquity if they were to somehow confront them. Our contemporary West is a culture inspired by the Semitic religions. In the context of our discussion, this cognitive shift away from Rome and towards Jerusalem is what constitutes the West, whether you're geographically located in the heart of Europe or in some university in Delhi. This may sound a bit cryptic right now, but as we talk about these things some more, you will see what I mean.

Arya: Fair enough. In any case, most of us are in agreement that Hinduism is not a religion. I guess it's just a matter of convenience now to refer to it as one. I understand that such descriptions originated with the missionaries and western scholars a few centuries ago. But Hindus have other concepts such as *dharma* which can be considered similar to religion. We just need to be able to describe our traditions more accurately using words from our own languages.

Leela: As I was at pains to point out earlier, the problem does not revolve around the words we use. If you challenge the Hindus on this point, it's typical of them to respond by saying, "when I say 'religion', I mean *dharma*; when I say 'God', I mean *Brahman*, when I say salvation, I mean *moksha*." You have no idea how nonsensical all of this really is. There is nothing even remotely similar in the Indian traditions that could correspond to the conceptualization of God in the Semitic religions. Their God is the Creator of the world, He has a will, and governs the world He has created in accordance with His purpose.

Reeti: We too have umpteen creation myths. In fact, creation is supposed to be a spontaneous activity of God – just as a blissful person spontaneously breaks into a song, God spontaneously creates the world.

Leela: Although our folklore is replete with creation myths, mulling over the origin of the universe has never been part of the Indian intellectual traditions. Creation is usually shrugged off as a *leela*, without any intent or purpose. In fact this is what the word 'spontaneous' suggests – something that is done without any intent or purpose. Contrast this with the Semitic conceptualization of God. If you say that God is a person whose will created and governs the universe, this means that everything that ever happened, is happening now, and that will happen in the future is His will. There is no possibility for Him to commit certain actions intentionally, while other actions are committed playfully, mischievously, or unintentionally.

Besides, the Biblical God is distinct and separate from the creatures He has created; He has plans and purposes in creation; His intention expresses itself as the laws of the Universe; we cannot know why He created the Universe; even when He tells us through His revelation why He did what He did, we do not understand it adequately, and so on. Taking these properties of God, it becomes clear that no being in the Indian traditions is God. None of these entities has the properties posited by the Semitic conceptualization of God, no matter how the texts from Sanskrit get translated and no matter how we ourselves use the word 'god'.

Reeti: Well, I have to agree that even though people in the West act like they are free to conceive of God in whatever manner suits them, all of their conceptualizations are actually confined within very narrow limits. For one thing, their God has to be good and perfect. Nor do they regard any tree or mountain to be God. Animals are out too. I suppose it's something we've never sat down to think about, but if God is supposed to be someone who creates the universe and has a will that governs it, then naturally He cannot be a lake, or a serpent, or a grain of rice. I see now what you mean when you say that this is more a result of unreflective translation and cannot possibly be an accurate mapping of the Indian concept of *deva* or *Ishwara* on to the Christian one of God.

Leela: We've merely learned this way of talking in response to questions like "What is your religion" and "What are your scriptures". However, by taking on the conceptual structures from Christian theology we only end up widening the already huge chasm between ourselves and our traditions.

Reeti: But what about all of our numerous scholarly tracts that speak of ethics and so on? Can these be considered to be our scriptures?

Leela: If a scholarly tract speaks of ethics, then it is an ethical tract; if it speaks of cosmology, it is a cosmological tract; if it speaks of self-knowledge, then it is a psychological tract; if it tells stories, then it is a mythological tract. The only reason we call them religious tracts or scriptures is because our colonial masters picked out certain texts, deemed them to be our religious texts, and taught us to repeat after them that these are our scriptures. Now one of the most insidious problems we have on our hands is that most Indians have begun transforming the Indian traditions into a religion that resembles Christianity as closely as possible. In fact, I believe that the Hindus of New Jersey and California have even drafted a list of the Hindu Ten Commandments that they dutifully feed to their children. These Hindus will be the first to jump up and down about the way western ethnographers describe their traditions, but they don't notice how absurd they themselves are being. The postcolonial Indian intellectuals seem to believe that placing the Indian traditions on a par with a religion such as Christianity is the only way to 'save Hinduism'. I am convinced that taking this course is bound to obstruct us from gaining any real knowledge of what the Indian traditions are.

Arya: Okay, what then is Hinduism if it is not a religion?

Leela: This way of looking at the problem is misguided and will not help us understand the Indian traditions. Your question presupposes that there is a recognizable phenomenon of Hinduism in the world. You can accept this proposition only if you also accept that there is something common to all the practices and traditions we designate as Hinduism. Bear in mind that, way back in the colonial times, western scholars began the task of trying to identify the beliefs and practices of Hinduism. It's been three hundred years and so far no-one has been successful in being able to identify the structure that distinguishes Hinduism from other social phenomena in Indian society. As the textbooks on Hinduism repeat time after time, no single doctrine or practice can be found that is accepted by all so-called Hindus or Hindu traditions. The belief that there is a phenomenon of Hinduism in Indian society does not have any theoretical or empirical foundation.

Arya: But there is no single doctrine that is accepted by all Christians, Jews or Muslims either!

Leela: That's not true. To a Muslim, Mohammed is a prophet, the Koran is the divine message, Allah is God, idolatry is a sin, and there are definite ways of worshipping God. Similar constraints apply to the Jews and Christians. One way to test whether some doctrine is common to these religions is to formulate negative questions: Could a Jew remain a Jew if he accepted that Jesus is the Christ? Could a Muslim remain a Muslim if he denied that Mohammed is the prophet of God? Of course there are different interpretations of the doctrines within these religions. But this is because of a conflict in interpreting the *commonly accepted* divine message. The conflict is not caused by an inability to identify the message. Not only that, there are limits to interpretation: you can never provide an interpretation that negates the divine message. In other words, in Christianity, Satan cannot be your object of worship under any interpretation. Contrast this with the Indian traditions where the status of Ravana and Rama may differ depending upon the region you are in, and the fact that some of the *rakshasas* and *asuras* are venerated during festivals.

Arya: But you cannot deny that there are many practices that are commonly-held among Hindus all over the world!

Leela: Well then, go ahead and tell me what I have to do in order to become a Hindu. If people across the length and breadth of India identify themselves as Hindus, but there is no single practice common to them, the question of practice is an illegitimate one. We can always find common practices at one level or another, from the brushing of teeth to the wearing of bangles or the eating of rice. But such practices do not make someone into a religious being called a Hindu. Isn't this the question at stake? Unless we can identify at least one practice which makes someone a Hindu there is no need to go looking for common properties.

Reeti: We all cremate our dead, get married around a fire altar, and have similar ceremonies all across India to mark the different stages of life.

Leela: But again, how does any of this add up to being religious? Many of these are practices are done out of sheer practical considerations. Besides, over the course of the centuries, people have come to realize the enormous significance of certain events in a human life. Birth, death, marriage and harvests are examples of some of the events that people deemed worthy of being solemnized or celebrated. This has nothing to do with beliefs, doctrine or religion. It's almost like saying that blowing out candles on a birthday cake is a religious practice just because it is a common practice among certain sets of people. In fact, it is quite normal to find these types of nonsensical descriptions of Hindu beliefs and practices that assert how all of Hindu life is permeated by religion.

Arya:　Okay, if religion is an inadequate word, what other word or concept captures the breadth and depth of Hinduism?

Leela:　Here we go again with words and meanings! Words like 'Hinduism', 'Buddhism', or 'Jainism' do not have any reference to a phenomena where the claim is that *such words name a religion*. Hinduism is basically a conceptual scheme imposed by our colonial masters upon social, cultural and traditional phenomena that exist in India. The idea of Hinduism imposes an imaginary unity upon varied sets of ritual practices, traditional stories, theoretical speculations, and art-forms that are present in Indian society. It then tries to relate these practices to a set of equally imaginary beliefs which are vaguely based on the stories and theoretical speculations of some of the Indian traditions.

Reeti:　But surely people from the West were seeking a genuine understanding of our traditions, so why did they complicate matters by concocting imaginary entities?

Leela:　Western culture is constituted by the dynamic of Christianity. When people from this type of culture describe peoples from other cultures, they do so based upon their own conceptual compulsion. This compulsion forces them to construct entities which lend stability and structure to their experience. So, for example, they take elements present in India, weave them into a pattern and this lends intelligibility to their experience. However, it does not make sense to us. While each of the elements that go into weaving the pattern does exist in India, taken together, this pattern does not describe the structure of Indian society or culture. The choice of elements that go into the weaving of this pattern is not random: only some elements are selected and others discarded. This suggests that western descriptions of India were guided by a theory. This 'theory' is Christian theology. Indians have come to accept these descriptions as descriptions of Indian culture and society. They are not. They are reports of the experience of the people who come from cultures constituted by the dynamic of their religions.

Reeti: So your basic objection is that all of the facts exist but they are not related to each other in a way that unites them into a single phenomenon that can be called a religion?

Leela: Precisely. The *puja* and the temples exist. The *mantras* and the notions of *dharma* and *adharma* exist. Rituals and practices exist. However, the unified entity created by tying these things together is the problem. This unity is a unity for the western world. Their descriptions are not based on a perverse wish to distort the descriptions of other cultures. There is simply no other way that they can look at the world. They are conceptually compelled to look at them in this way.

Reeti: What do you mean? How do these conceptual compulsions get in the way?

Leela: Consider, for example, that up until the last century, in Europe and America it was *believable* that people had sex with the devil. There were eye-witnesses who testified to this in courts of law. From a twenty-first century perspective, we find this hard to understand and would regard such assertions as being outright lies or hallucinations at best. But another way to understand this is to consider how the beliefs of these people were structured. Their religion had convinced them that the devil exists and this belief was held to be true. This made it plausible for them to attest to the fact that they had seen the devil. In other words, when we perceive something in the world, our perception is not merely the result of processing all of the stimulus cues that come at us. It also involves fitting our prior knowledge to the current situation. The things we already know influence what we see.

It is easy to write off all western scholarship on India and other cultures as racist, Orientalist, or Eurocentric. However, the way I prefer to approach the problem is to try and find out what background presuppositions these scholars were working with. When Europeans set out to discover India, the Biblical framework shaped their horizon of expectations. They took it for granted that religion existed everywhere in the world and therefore also in India. This is what the Bible tells them and this is what they believed to be the truth. They brought with them a specific idea of religion and then tried to fit various things that they saw and experienced in India into this idea of religion that they brought with them. Their idea of religion included such things as doctrine, prophets, scriptures and the notion of God. It did not take long for the European scholars and missionaries to discover that Hindus did not have any fixed notion of doctrines or scriptures or prophets or even a God. Instead of coming to the conclusion that what they saw in India could not be religion at all, they insisted on declaring that in spite of the fact that there is no concept of God or scripture common to Hindus, Hinduism is a religion nonetheless. To them, the question whether religion exists in someplace was never a matter of empirical investigation because it was theoretically so certain that no investigation seemed necessary.

Arya: It is certainly possible that this is what happened. But I would say that it is closer to our modern experience that they merely described a unitary phenomenon the wrong way. Certain things about Indian culture, such as the festivals, fasts, temples, shrines, *puja*, pilgrimage, and the epics can well be considered to indicate a unitary phenomenon that goes by the name of Hinduism.

Leela: Perhaps the best way to make some headway in this discussion is to get back to the basics for a moment. Many facts are interconnected within a culture. Based on some theory or the other, we can pick out certain facts and provide an explanation for these facts. This explanation helps us understand the phenomenon in question because the theory under discussion is able to show what the interconnection between the facts is. The theory tells us about the pattern that unifies these facts into a whole of some sort.

Now the question is this: which facts are relevant? When you come up with your laundry list of facts, you provide a very particular list of practices, epics, shrines, and so on. These facts, and not other facts, such as the structure of the village courtyards, the weekly vegetable bazaar, or the recipe for *idlis*, are considered relevant to deciding what Hinduism is. That you select only some facts as relevant facts to discuss the nature of Hinduism suggests that you are working with an implicit (or explicit) theory or idea about what religion is. Only a theory can assign weights and relevance to facts. If you were to have no background theory about what Hinduism is, you would simply wave your hands in the direction of India and say that all the facts of the culture have a pattern behind them and that pattern is Hinduism.

Reeti: I think I get it now. You're saying that Hinduism-as-a-religion picks out the same elements as Hinduism-as-something-but-not-a-religion picks out. We too have fallen into the religious trap.

Leela: Thanks Reeti, it's good to know I've not just been howling in the wind. I'm just trying to make the following simple point. In choosing some facts as relevant facts, one uses a theory. All facts, to put it even more simply, are facts of a theory. The existence question of Hinduism can come up only in the presence of a theory, whether explicit or implicit. If we are not careful, we merely take over the commonly-held conceptions of Christianity to identify Hinduism, even if we explicitly say that it is not a religion.

Reeti: Wait, what do you mean when you say that all facts are facts of a theory? The fact that I wear a sari or a *bindi* are facts in themselves and do not belong to any theory.

Leela: It is not the case that there are any neutral 'facts' floating around that we must first collect and then proceed to explain. Depending on the context, say a discussion about some aspect of Indian culture, folks can treat wearing a *bindi* or a sari as simple facts. However, in a different context, these facts might become theoretical claims. Consider, for instance, the legislation in some countries against wearing religious symbols in public. In a dispute along these lines, if someone decides to take a Hindu to court, wearing a *bindi* or *kumkum* will be treated as facts within a theory. One side will claim that these are religious symbols, and the other side will say that they are not. In such a case, wearing a *bindi* will be described from within two different theoretical frameworks. In any situation, we need to differentiate between facts and theory as the context requires. There are no theory-neutral facts for scientific theories to explain and it is not a matter of going about collecting facts in order to explain them.

Reeti: I see now why you said that words like 'religion', 'worship', 'sacred' and 'god' cannot be neutral observational terms but are theoretical terms embedded in the framework of Christian theology.

Leela: Precisely. This background framework provides meaning to these terms and relates them to each other in a conceptual grid. Similarly, statements like 'every culture has a religion', 'Brahmins are the priests of Hinduism' or 'Buddhism was a reform movement against Brahmanism' are not factual or historical observations, but theoretical statements generated by this same Christian-theological framework.

Arya: But how do you explain the fact that even luminaries like Gandhi and Vivekananda referred to Hinduism as a religion and said things like "all religions are true."

Leela: Don't forget the impact of centuries of colonization on all of us. This has had a significant effect on Indian thinkers. From what I have read of Vivekananda, I am convinced that he did not have any idea of the nature and magnitude of the problem he was up against. As members of the Hindu traditions, they tend to share the pagan attitude which relates the 'truth' of religion to its tradition and its practices. However, nowadays we are increasingly beginning to share the Christian attitude which relates religious truth to the theological proof one has for doctrines and beliefs.

Arya: There's another problem though. If cognitive schemes are as deep-rooted as you say, then wouldn't any attempts taken by Hindus to reinterpret their traditions also result in some type of distortion?

Leela: But there can always be breakthroughs! After all, the rishis, gurus and swamis have reinterpreted the Indian traditions throughout Indian history. There were cross-fertilizations between the Indian traditions that generated new and very creative insights as exemplified by Buddhism, the tantric traditions, and the *Bhakti* traditions. Contrast this with the contemporary yoga explosion in the West. For all the dedication and excellence of the practitioners, it has not been accompanied by any cognitive breakthrough. Instead, everything they say sounds like dogma and doctrine. They interpret the Indian traditions as embodying doctrines and belief systems because this is the only way they know how to look at things.

Arya: Frankly, I'm so used to thinking in terms of beliefs myself that I cannot wrap my head around any alternative way of thinking.

Leela: Our traditions do not revolve around doctrines and beliefs. Ritual practices and reflections on experience are their central concerns. Texts are important only insofar as they assist such ritual practices and experiential reflections. The reinterpretations of, say, a Shankara were creative because they generated new reflections on human experience. The western reinterpretation, on the contrary, stifles all creativity because it transforms traditions into something that they are not: fixed doctrines or belief systems. Sadly, now it's the same scenario in India. Gone is the tradition of truly reflecting on your experience. Interpretation now takes a form similar to disputes between different Christian theologians. Scholars are transformed into dry pundits without being able to make any original contribution to the regeneration of Indian culture. There are pundits upon pundits all over the place and hardly any gurus.

Reeti: There's something paradoxical about this whole scenario. I mean, on one hand, India is one of the few pagan cultures left in the world which means that it stood its ground in some way. On the other hand, we are completely out of touch with our own traditions, which is odd for a culture that has managed to survive.

Leela: Yes, it is indeed a strange paradox that would be well worth studying. The acceptance of 'Hinduism' as a real entity in Indian society has had important consequences and lasting effects on our society. Even though it is difficult to alter our way of thinking, we need to make an effort to do so if we want to get out of this quagmire. It's best to do away with the question whether Hinduism, be it a religion or not-religion exists or not. We need to pitch this at some other level of abstraction, say, for example, a theory of cultural difference, or how different cultures are structured, and then to try and figure out the way in which Indian culture differs from western culture. This is the task that confronts us.

My approach has been to try and discover whether it is possible to show that there is a common set of problems which the Indian traditions have tried to solve. We will need to study Indian ethics and contrast it with the nature of western ethics. We will need to go deeper into some of the *Bhakti* traditions. We will need to reformulate questions about *avidya* and *gyana udaya* using twenty-first century language and theories. Then we can try and figure out whether such a procedure is going to yield a new pattern but one which will not be confused with religion. Not only do I believe that a different description is possible but also that it will be cognitively superior to the prevailing view.

Arya: In that case, if it is an open question, the results of our research may well turn out to show that there is a pattern in our culture that can be called Hinduism!

Leela: Evolutionary biology does not disprove the existence of unicorns in the world. Is this any reason to prefer the story about the virgin and the unicorn over evolutionary biology? All I can do is draw your attention to how theories are assessed and leave it at that. I do not have any knock-down philosophical arguments that can meet every possible kind of objection. If this is not enough, I cannot do much about it.

Reeti: Please don't get into a huff. In any case, this is what we've been saying too in some way or another – that there is a pan-Indian cultural phenomenon that does not fit into the category of religion and we want to learn how to talk about it.

Leela: Why not just define 'Hindus' as those who use *garam masala* in their cuisine? You will surely find a cohesive, unified phenomenon that will cover the length and breadth of India. We can have discussions along these lines forever and never reach any reasonable conclusion.

Arya: I think we are truly going around in circles now. We need to get out of this quagmire of our own before anything else.

Reeti: I agree. We are not making any headway and tempers are starting to fray. The immediate question we want to resolve is: what is the framework by which we can study the shared cultural experience, practices, and traditions that we find across India? It's fine to say that we haven't figured out how to describe it as yet, but we cannot trivialize this absence of an explanation.

CHAPTER III

THE MEANING OF LIFE

Arya: It's unfortunate that we ended on such a crotchety note yesterday. It occurred to me that we could have avoided going around in circles if we'd started out with a proper definition of religion.

Leela: Then you'll be disappointed to learn that the hallways of academia are littered with rejected definitions of the word 'religion'. Of course that has never stopped others from coming up with yet more definitions, but none of these has helped bring about any clarity. You see, definitions don't explain anything. It's like putting a label on something without being able to provide any understanding of the matter. Even though we start out wanting to gain some knowledge about the subject, we end up merely talking about whether something can be classified as religion or not. The discussions for the past couple of centuries have not progressed beyond debates as to which entities we can include under the term 'religion' and how far out on a limb we want to go in considering whether to include things such as football, voodoo, or Marxism under this classification. This type of a classificatory exercise is not the same as acquiring knowledge about a subject. Any dispute about definitions is like a conflict of tastes; the discussions are interminable and yield no knowledge.

Arya: I suppose this is similar to trying to decide whether a whale is a fish or a mammal based on a definition. There is no way to settle this kind of a dispute without a theoretical framework that conceptualizes the distinct properties of fishes and other animals. Evolutionary biology provides us with a framework that allows us to distinguish fishes from mammals in terms of the way in which they procreate or breathe oxygen from the air. This settles the debate and we are not left with interminable, fruitless disputes.

Leela: Precisely. That is why we need to develop a theoretical framework to understand religion. In fact, I have been busy developing one such framework. My framework demonstrates that either Judaism, Christianity and Islam are religions or the Indian traditions are religions. Both statements cannot be true at the same time – in the same way that both fishes and whales cannot belong to the same species within the framework of evolutionary biology.

Right now there is huge inconsistency that exists in the field of religious studies. Judaism, Christianity and Islam have fixed doctrines, Holy Scriptures, and ecclesiastical structures that are *necessary properties* for these religions. For example, if there was no Bible, no Jesus, and no church, Christianity would not exist in any recognizable form that would allow us to identify it as a religion. By contrast, the Hindu, Buddhist, Jain, Tao, Shinto, the Native American traditions, etc., do not have these properties. Yet they are distinguishable entities in themselves and are also distinguishable from each other. If such properties are *necessary properties* for religion, then Hinduism must have them too. But the Indian and other traditions do not have these properties, and yet they can be distinguished from one another. This goes to show that we have two different kinds of phenomena at hand.

Arya: Aren't such determinations best left to theologians? Surely they can give us a better idea about religion than any theory a non-believer could come up with?

Leela: Not really. We are trying to understand what *religion* is and not what Christianity is. To figure out what makes something into a religion, we need to develop a hypothesis about religion that is independent of theology.

Reeti: Okay, I see where you're going with this. It's no use trying to define religion since that exercise is fruitless in terms of providing knowledge. So we need to develop a theory that can shed light on this concept. Perhaps things will become clearer once you elaborate on the theory that you are developing.

Leela: As a first step, we need to fix a reference for the word 'religion' so we can know what we are talking about when we use this word. One of the accepted procedures for defining a word is by pointing to the object it refers to. A child, for example, learns what a 'cat' is by pointing out a cat and not by teaching it that a cat is a furry, four-legged animal. It is a fairly safe bet to point to Christianity as a prototypical example of religion, just so that we can fix a reference for the word. Christianity self-identifies as a religion, so the choice of picking it as a prototypical example of religion is not arbitrary. Irrespective of whether Hinduism or Buddhism or Football or Voodoo can be considered religions, Christianity is a religion if the word 'religion' refers to anything at all.

Arya: Now that we've fixed a reference for the term 'religion' it still doesn't explain what religion is except that it tells us that Christianity is an example of one.

Leela: That's right. Fixing the reference is merely a first step that allows us to proceed further. It is worth noting that just because some properties of Christianity are absent from Hinduism, we cannot, on this basis, conclude that Hinduism is not a religion. We will be justified in saying this only if we are able to show that the properties of religion are the properties of Christianity, and that Hinduism does not have these properties. Since we have not determined the properties of religion as yet, all we can do at this stage is notice that Christianity and some other traditions differ from each other. Once we have fully developed our theory, then based upon the implications and consequences of our theory we will be in a position to state whether Hinduism, Buddhism, Jainism, and other traditions are religions or not. Like all proper scientific hypotheses, our hypothesis should be able to be tested in a number of ways.

Reeti: How do you go about testing something as abstract as this?

Leela: To start with, any hypothesis on religion must make sense of the facts as they played out in history. Secondly, it should be able to account for the various aspects of religion as they appear to those who are religious. Finally, since I claim that the pagan and heathen traditions are different phenomena from religion, the hypothesis must be able to show how their response to Christianity reflects this difference. These are the historical and experiential constraints that we must operate within if we wish to generate a theory of religion. The test of our theory must show that it fits within these constraints.

Arya: Okay. So far we've established that we can take Christianity to be a prototypical example of religion and that it has certain necessary properties like God, the Bible and churches. Now you need to show us how you can weave these facts into a series of interrelated hypotheses within the historical constraints and in keeping with how people experience religion.

Leela: History tells us that Christianity described itself and other traditions as 'religion'. Moreover, the terms under which Christianity recognized itself as a religion are also the terms under which Islam and Judaism recognized themselves as religions. History also tells us that these entities not only recognized each other as religions, but also regarded each other as *rival* religions. Christianity was intolerant of both heretics and heathens and persecuted beliefs and practices that ran counter to those of its own.

By contrast, neither the Roman cults that flourished at the time of the birth of Christianity, nor the Indian traditions that Christianity later encountered, recognized themselves in the Christian descriptions of their traditions. They reacted with incomprehension about the fact that different traditions could be rivals in this sense. These historical facts provide us with a launching pad to begin our study of religion and can also serve as a way to test the theory once it is developed. If my theory of religion can explain all of these facts, it would mean that the theory encompasses both the Abrahamic conception of religion shared by Judaism, Christianity and Islam, and the pagan conception of tradition, shared by the ancient Romans, the Indian, and other traditions.

Arya: Wait a minute. History also tells us that these religions have had many types of rivals, such as monarchies, democracies, dictatorships, and communism. While these are rivals to religion, they cannot be called religious rivals. How can we make a distinction between different kinds of rivals if we don't know what properties make something a religion?

Leela: An excellent point, and one on which I actually rely upon to build my theory. If we can find out on what basis Christianity regarded some entity to be a religious rival, as opposed to any other kind of rival, this would give us *its* conception of religion. Then we can build upon that. So, to begin with, Christians noted differences in beliefs or doctrines. They believed that the actions of the faithful are embodiments of their beliefs. Consequently, conversion from one religion to another meant a rejection of one set of beliefs and embracing another set of beliefs on the grounds of truth and falsity.

Reeti: What kind of beliefs and doctrine are we talking about?

Leela: The doctrines specifically revolved around anything that had to do with God and his relationship to humanity. Thus, as a first step in the characterization of religion we can say that it involves an emphasis on doctrines or beliefs, and it regards actions as embodiments of these beliefs. These facts are what we need to account for in our conceptualization of religion. We must be able to explain religious rivalry, the necessity of God to religion, and the importance of doctrine.

Reeti: Got it.

Leela: To get a better grip on what comes next, I think I should first set the stage by talking about a problem from the social sciences. This problem revolves around the distinction between causes and reasons. Say, we want to know why the sky is blue. We can open up our books and learn about light and wavelengths, the retina, color, and the whole host of interrelated hypotheses that explain why the sky is blue. These are the causes that make the sky blue. But if we want to know for what reason the sky is blue, there can be no answer other than say, it's because God willed it to be so, or maybe it's for the reasons in that story your grandmother told you....

Reeti: But there is no real reason why the sky is blue, except for the causal reasons!

Leela: Okay, let's look at another example. Say, you ask me: "Why are you a Professor?" In one sense the 'why' refers to the cause, that is, the answer might be that I have been appointed as one by the governing Council of the University. In another sense the 'why' refers to my intention: because I want to do research and teach. Thus, we have two types of answers to the same question: one has to do with the causes that explain how something takes place, and the other has to do with the reasons that make things intelligible by appealing to intentions.

Arya: Isn't this what the gap between the social sciences and the natural sciences revolves around? The natural sciences, say, can explain why someone is obese in terms of the biological causes of obesity, while the social sciences would provide reasons based on psychological, behavioral, or socio-economic factors, that might explain the condition.

Leela: Exactly. While it is relatively simple to work out the cause of something in the world, it's not possible to infer the intentions of somebody simply by looking at their actions. This is because the same action might express different intentions. For example, I may shut a window because I feel the room is getting cold, or because there's too much noise on the street, or perhaps I'm afraid that bugs will get in. There's no way of knowing why I shut the window merely by observing the fact that I shut it. Thus, we cannot understand someone's behavior by trying to infer their belief states or intentional states as they are called. To complicate things further, our actions often have unintended effects and it is always the case that we might not be able to realize our intentions. There isn't any one-on-one correspondence between our intentions and our actions since the 'world' happens to get in the way of our plans. This, in a nutshell, is what we need to know about the distinction between causes and reasons and the gap between intentions and actions.

Reeti: Are we still talking about religion? Just want to make sure I'm not totally missing something.

Leela: Yes, and we're ready to get back on track now. What religion does is the following: It introduces an agent – God – and tells us that the intentions of this agent and the regularities in nature (say, causes) fall together. To put it simply, religion tells us that God created the universe and the universe is an expression of God's will. In other words, God is the cause of the universe and he is also the reason for the universe. Moreover, religion tells us that God is perfect and His will and His actions correspond perfectly. Therefore, unlike us earthly creatures who must live with the fact that our intentions do not necessarily find expression in our actions, God's actions are a perfect expression of His will. Because God is perfect and everything he intends takes place exactly as he wills, by looking at his actions we can draw inferences about the reasons for His actions. The only problem is that we can never provide a complete description of the purposes of God because we cannot possibly observe all His actions.

However, we have two sources of knowledge: a set of actions that we can try to understand, and a message that we can try to make sense of. The set of actions is all of God's creation, that is, the Cosmos. The message is His Revelation, that is, the Bible. We now have on our hands what we can call a 'religious doctrine'. In providing such an account, religion gives us an explanation for the universe that can answer the 'why' question in both its senses. "Why does the universe exist?" It is because God created it. Or, "why does the universe exist?" Because it is an expression of God's purpose. The fact that God created the universe for a reason infuses the world with meaning. The religious account thus structures our experience in such a way that we experience the universe as something that can be explained and made sense of. In a deep and fundamental sense, to grow up within a religious culture is to grow up with this type of experience.

Reeti: I don't think I understand the last part too well. What sense are we supposed to make of the universe?

Leela: This doctrine does not actually explain the Cosmos or make it intelligible. Rather, it merely affirms that the universe is such a place. To better grasp this claim, it may help to contrast it with the Indian concept of *leela* which suggests quite the opposite – that it is futile to look for intelligibility in the events in the Cosmos. This is not the case with religion because the religious account is a truth claim. It makes a truth claim by saying that the universe is the expression of the purposes of God. Therefore, if you want knowledge of the universe, the knowledge must take the form of an account that explains and makes sense of the universe. This account is God's revelation and is contained in the Bible. By claiming that God's revelation is contained in the Bible, religion makes *itself* intelligible as well. It tells us that the Bible is the word of God, and we know this because the Bible says so. In this sense, religion is self-reflexive, meaning that it refers to itself. Its truth rests on its own foundation. This is why religion is not a human invention – it is God's gift to humanity. All of these ideas taken together are what make an explanation into a 're-ligious' explanation.

Arya: So basically the religious account is a form of an explanation that fuses causes and reasons and includes itself as part of the purposes of God. I suppose I can understand how this type of doctrine can shape our beliefs about the world, but I'm skeptical about why God is *necessary* in all of this. After all, if we are to believe in a perfect entity like God, why can't we just believe in the Flying Spaghetti Monster with a will of its own, or why not one of our own capricious gods? We'd have a lot less explaining to do if God wasn't all perfect and good.

Leela: This has to do with the kind of beings we humans are and the fact that the religious account makes a truth claim. In other words, these are the anthropological constraints on the religious account. The account must work for us as human beings, with human methods of learning, and with mechanisms of transmission in human societies. Remember, religion is an intentional explanation, that is to say, it appeals to beliefs and reasons. It tells us that God made the universe for a reason, and to find out the reasons, He gave us the Revelation, or the Bible.

Reeti: What reasons does religion talk about?

Leela: Human beings were created as sentient beings to worship God and obey Him. This is the 'reason' to worship God. His commandment is to worship only Him and only in the way He has specified. I don't mean to get too technical, but to fully address the question about why God is necessary to religion we need to examine the notion of intentionality and its relation to intelligibility in some detail. Intentionality refers to the 'aboutness' of things such as hopes, desires, and plans. In other words, our hopes and desires are always about something. You dream *about* a vacation, or you're sad *about* someone's illness.

When we talk about beliefs, 'intelligibility' refers to the meaning of that belief. When we say that a belief, or a story, or a theory, is intelligible, we mean that it is understandable. Without the notion of an agent with intentions there can be no intelligibility to this account. That is why God has to be a person in this account. God must be good and perfect to work within the anthropological constraints of religion in human societies. And that is why any old Spaghetti Monster won't do as a replacement for God.

Reeti: I think that all of us use intentional explanations so how is it specifically related to religion or God? Our intentions are always about something. I mean, if I ask "why did you carry your umbrella to work", you would say because you expected it to rain, and you did not want to get wet, which would be expressions of what you believe and wish.

Leela: Of course, all human being have beliefs, hopes and desires. However, religion claims something more than that. It fuses the 'why' questions and their answers, with the 'how' questions and their answers. The 'how' and the 'why' questions are answered by one and the same thing: God's will. This will is the causal structure of the cosmos, and this will is also the reason for the cosmos. For example, God made the gravitational force, and the reason the gravitational force exists is because God wants the cosmos to be this way. Natural laws are seen as expressions of the constancy of God's will. In fact, this is one of the reasons why science emerged in religious cultures. Studying God's will was to understand the 'how' of the regularities in the Cosmos. Religion explains or answers the 'how' questions and while doing so, it also makes the Cosmos intelligible. In no other realm of human existence do the 'how' and the 'why' questions fuse together. They do so only in religion. An intentional account of *human* actions could never live up to this demand since there is an inevitable discrepancy between the causes and reasons in the human case. We are never able to realize all of our intentions.

Arya: Just to back up a little. I thought science and religion were completely opposed to each other. How can it be that religion gave birth to science?

Leela: Well, such disputes themselves were responsible for the growth of scientific theorizing in the West. The discussion about the age of the earth, for example, was a controversy within religious discourse itself. The threat of atheism and heresy fueled the debates about the age of the earth, which was to ultimately provide us with geology, paleontology and so on. Religion related phenomena to each other – the Cosmos to the individual; actions to beliefs; individuals to society – and provided the ground for all of these in one single postulate: the God of the Bible was the fountainhead of everything. This doctrine provided an explanatory link between phenomena otherwise unconnected by appealing to an invisible ordering force. The dissemination of this belief among all layers of the population for more than a thousand years is absolutely unique to religion. The typical belief that grounded the basic attitude of the West for centuries was the idea that the Cosmos could be explained and made intelligible. Because this intelligibility was not evident to the senses, it required a search for the underlying explanatory units. In other words, what we call a scientific attitude today is continuous with the religious attitude. Religion formed it, nurtured it, and gave birth to science as a result. Religion, then, provides us with the most fundamental model of what it is for something to be an explanation. It links parts of the world to each other by postulating necessary and intelligible connections between them. This is the reason why the natural sciences emerged in religious cultures – among the Jews and Christians – and why they failed to emerge in, say, China.

Reeti: I do have to say that this picture of God being perfectly consistent and reliable is in stark contrast to the stories from our traditions. The only thing consistent about our gods is their unpredictability and their meddlesomeness.

Leela: By contrast, the Bible inculcates an experience of the Cosmos as a particular kind of order where things express a deep, underlying constancy. This constancy is the will of God that governs the world. To accept this is to accept that everything in the universe has a purpose. Since our birth and death occur in the Cosmos, consequently these events have a purpose as well. To be part of a religion is to believe that human life and death (and everything in between) have significance, a meaning, and a purpose. A religious doctrine need not specify the purpose of any individual life or death; it is enough to merely say that there is one. Consequently, to accept that life, including your life, has a meaning and a purpose is to accept this doctrine. It means believing in the fact that your life itself can be explained and made intelligible. This does not imply that any particular religion must have a specific statement to the effect that the Cosmos is an entity that can be explained and made intelligible. This is, nevertheless, the affirmation provided by religion. It makes the world into such a place by structuring the experience of the world accordingly – we view the world from within such a framework.

Arya: But can we not say that the Indian traditions also concern themselves with meaning and purpose? The *Upanishads* address such concerns as life and death and these can very well be seen to carry aspects of the meaning questions of the West.

Leela: All meaning questions are basically about a 'why' that picks out a reason for an action or an event. The meaning of human existence, insofar as we construe it as a 'why' question, asks: why do we exist? One obvious answer is to refer to the procreative acts of our parents. The other is to talk about the reasons for our existence, that is, to specify why we are put on earth. In the Indian traditions, I have not found any group of people or texts that speak in such terms. Even those who speak of a creator, speak of creation as a *leela*, not as an expression of the plans or reasons of the creator. In the Abrahamic religions, by contrast, the entire Universe exhibits the plan and order that God intends and wills. That is why it makes sense in western culture to ask questions about the meaning of life. In the Indian traditions, this is not considered a well-formed question and there is almost no speculation along these lines.

Reeti: Actually this comes as quite a relief to me. I've never been able to relate to the 'meaning of life' question. I always thought I was missing something.

Leela: No religion has been able to answer a specific individual's existential questions. In fact, if you talk to people who believe that they have found the meaning and purpose in life, you get the following reply: they describe what they are doing, and inform you that this description is the meaning of their lives. In other words, they merely assert that the meaning of life is the life that they are leading. They may say, for example, that they pursue the arts, spend time with their kids, or use their skills to help the needy and this brings meaning to their lives. Even though what we have on our hands is a mere re-description of their actions, this account makes it intelligible.

The answer to the question of the meaning of life cannot be sought by trying to answer this question. The problem lies elsewhere, namely, in the belief that allows you to ask such a question in the first place. If religion was really invented as an answer to such questions as 'Why am I born?', 'Where am I going?', 'What is the meaning or purpose of life?' why would religious figures like Christ or Muhammad have kept silent about it? The answer is simple. Religion does not answer these questions nor has it ever answered them. What it does is enable us to raise such questions. Religion was not invented to answer questions about the meaning and purpose of life. These questions come into being within the framework of religion. They are generated by religion. Take religion away and these questions will go away too.

Reeti: Actually, if you think about it, there's a lot to suggest that the western experience is structured by the idea of meaning. "Everything happens for a reason" is an oft-heard phrase. Even the attitude towards art reflects this obsession with meaning. Every piece of art gets over-analyzed. It's as if talking and writing about art is as important as making or enjoying it. Anyway, to move on, I'd like to understand how the actual story of the Bible ties into the doctrines of Christianity. I'm trying to re-think religion in terms of how it structures our thoughts.

Leela: In a nutshell, the story is this: There was once a religion, the true and universal one, which was God's gift to all mankind. A sense of divinity was instilled in all individuals, everywhere in the world, by the creator God himself. During the course of human history, this sense was corrupted, and idolatry or devil worship began to prevail. Then God spoke to Abraham, Isaac and Jacob and led their tribe back on to the true path. God made a covenant with the people of Israel that He would send someone to liberate them. According to Christianity, the Christ figure is this promised one. The Christians claim that the Christ came not just to deliver the people of Israel but the whole of mankind. Only by following Christ can one hope to be delivered from the clutches of the devil. This is the notion of salvation, which has nothing to do with *moksha* or *nirvana*.

Now, of equal importance in this story is the devil. According to the religious account, all other gods are the minions of this devil. That is why we need to be saved from the clutches of all these false gods, because the only result of us worshipping them is eternal torture in Hell. From this perspective, you may think that Ganesha and Shiva are manifestations of God, but you would be deceived in this belief by the devil himself. In other words, you need to keep the devil as much in the front and center as God Himself. If you can understand the above account and not fall back on some old Hindu heathen interpretation to make sense of it, you are beginning to grasp what religion is. There's no use carrying on that *dharma* is religion, Jesus was a *yogi*, *leela* is God's will, revelation is an *avatar*, and all of the arrant nonsense that we carry on with. In this way we do justice neither to other cultures nor our own.

Arya: That seems a bit harsh and exaggerated. You've mentioned it innumerable times, but frankly I've never heard anyone speak of devil worship. And by the way, isn't it insulting to refer to Hindus as heathens or pagans?

Leela: It's insulting only if you accept the religious account according to which pagans and heathens are worshippers of false gods. To me it is just a convenient way of distinguishing between religious cultures, that is, the ones with the 'true' God from the so-called heathen or pagan ones with the 'false gods'. You say you have not heard anyone speak of devil worship, but then you probably have not tried to find out anything about religion. The way the religious account is structured, the problem of true and false religion is *unsolvable*. Our societies may carry on talking about religious tolerance all they want, but in fact what they have managed to work out is a form of civic tolerance, not religious tolerance, even if they call it that.

Reeti: But if religion is as specific as you say it is, then why do religious scholars insist that all cultures have religion? Surely it is obvious that we have very different cultural phenomena in different parts of the world.

Leela: This is because of the way in which the religious account structures the belief system of people in religious cultures. Remember, the claim made by religion is that God gave religion to all of humanity; it's just that some parts of humanity got duped by the devil and forgot the true religion. This theological prediction that religion exists among all peoples continues to shape the expectations and experience of scholars. This account is presented as the truth and is believed to be true. Against the background of this theology, there are certain questions to which a negative reply is not allowed. Questions such as "Does God really exist?" or "Do all peoples have religion?" are some of these questions.

You see, theology has a peculiar relation to the empirical world. As a theory, it generates empirical impossibilities rather than empirical consequences. It tells you: "the theological prediction establishes that religion exists in all cultures and if you think that the empirical world refutes this then you must be wrong." Because religion presents itself as the revelation of God and not as a human account, its truth claims have a different status from the truth claims of human accounts.

Arya: Okay, I understand that the figure of God is necessary to religion because it is an intentional account that appeals to reason, and that doctrines and scriptures are similarly necessary. But all of these religions developed through a historical process, so I'm curious to find out if things could have turned out differently.

Leela: Since the religious account presents itself as a true account of the causes and reasons for the universe, certain properties begin to flow from this one fact. As human beings, we need to make sense of this true account by attributing certain qualities to this entity called God who created the universe. Thus God is a necessary property for religion. Contrast this with Buddhism and Jainism that dispense with the notion of God altogether. Christianity cannot do this because something (an event, action, object) is intelligible to us only if it is an expression of an agent with a will. That is the reason why God is conceptualized as a person, and not as an impersonal Brahma-type entity. Not only that, since religion makes the claim that human beings fulfill some purpose handed down by God, it must be possible for them to achieve that purpose otherwise there would be no intelligibility to the account. Hence, an eschatology, or a goal for humanity as a whole, is part of such a message and religion must postulate a relation between God and human beings.

Not only must religion speak of God's purposes, why human beings are here, and what their goal is, but also how this goal can be achieved. The way to achieve this goal is through worship. Worship is the means through which the religious account continues to retain its character to the believers. In worship, man expresses his faith in God and affirms that he is using the means required to be a part of the purposes of God. Worship involves seeing the Cosmos as part of God's reasons and purposes and doing what is required in order to continue to experience the Cosmos in this way.

Reeti: I suppose this is another reason that worship is different from *puja* because you cannot say that *puja* is about aligning our will with God's will. But then, how should we go about differentiating our traditions from religion?

Leela: Traditions revolve around a human search; they are human products, an expression of human striving. They are the ways, customs, habits and ceremonies as developed by a people. This is the huge gulf that separates the pagans and heathens from religion. One is the tradition of a people the other is God's gift to humanity. By looking at Christianity as a human way of finding a practical solution to whatever life brings, we heathens are doubly blind. We are blind to the claim that religion is the truth as revealed by God; and we are blind because we do not see that religion views itself as the true explanation underlying God's creation. This is the part that most Hindus seem incapable of understanding. As I explained, religion is a reflexive entity, that is, its truth rests on its own foundation. It is what it says about itself, and what it says about itself is the truth. As such, it is accessible only to those who are a part of such an account. It's in the very nature of religion that those who are not from a religious background are blind to its existence.

Reeti: What do you mean we're blind to its existence?

Leela: Like I said, Hindus think that religion is merely some sort of tradition. They don't understand that it is a set of teachings handed down by God himself and not authored by human beings. In this sense religion is the 'other' of tradition. The predicates 'true' and 'false' are inapplicable to a tradition because it is a set of practices.

When people from religious cultures described our traditions, they transformed the very terms of description by characterizing our traditions as a belief-guided and theoretically-founded set of practices. Our practices were provided with something they never had or ever needed – a theoretical foundation. The very same stories and legends that surrounded the collective practices of our traditions are now seen to form a theoretical basis for the tradition. Practices that were carried on simply because they were handed down from generation to generation are now seen as requiring reason, justification, meaning and purpose. The 'otherness' of our tradition has been effectively wiped out by transforming it into 'another'.

Reeti: Another what?

Leela: Another religion, of course. This is how we Hindus have come to believe that Hinduism is a religion. If we view our traditions simply as traditions we do not need to provide them with any theoretical foundation. However, when transformed into a religion, this tradition acquires a property it never had before: reflexivity. It begins to refer to itself in search of a 'deeper' foundation. The inconsistent myths and legends, or the practices that have been preserved from time immemorial, are seen to express a deeper truth. In simple terms, the basic mechanism in the spread of religion works by erasing the otherness of the other. The other is transformed into an image of itself, that is, into a religion. There is no 'other' to religion; there is merely another religion. This is how the heathens and pagans are incorporated into theology. The otherness of traditions disappears once it is cast into the framework of the reflexive entity that religion is. Then it becomes impossible to think that India does not have any indigenous religions.

Reeti: But why did we succumb to this idea at all since our traditions are older than religion?

Leela: It was a long process. Slowly but surely the colonized Indians began to accept the western descriptions of India and began to see and experience their culture differently. Where they had initially expressed total incomprehension, they began to draw parallels and to sketch a picture of 'Hinduism' that began to track the criteria supplied by the colonizers.

Arya: I suppose this same story was repeated among the natives of Africa, the Americas and Australia. I am beginning to see how all of this ties in together. Your theory certainly explains the difference in attitude that exists between the Abrahamic religions and the heathen cultures. And it fits in with the historical facts and experiential elements such worship.

Leela: It also helps to identify the structure that distinguishes religion from other social phenomena. It connects a series of concepts such as God, the will of God, doctrines, worship and faith to describe the object that religion is. This is very different from defining the word 'religion'.

Arya: The next step, then, is to show whether we can apply this concept of religion to Buddhism or Hinduism or whatever else. How can we test to see whether we can derive the same empirical consequences in other traditions as we see in the case of religion?

Leela: Historical research shows that our traditions reacted with complete indifference to debates about the truth and falsity of religion. They did not have an idea of a true God who has revealed his will in contrast with numerous false gods. They could not understand how factual historical evidence and logical consistency were relevant in assessing the value of traditional stories. Nor did they perceive any problems in regarding several traditions as 'true' at the same time. There is no entity like Hinduism or Buddhism structured around seeking intelligibility in the cosmos, or trying to decipher God's will. Nor are these traditions obsessed with the 'meaning of life' questions. My theory of religion answers two questions simultaneously: what is the nature of religion and why do western intellectuals see religion in every culture? One of the problems I have tried to solve is why western culture assumes that every culture must have a religion.

Reeti: And that's because their scripture tells them that God gave religion to all of humanity? It's unfortunate that we ourselves are now hell-bent on transforming our multiple traditions into a single 'religion' called Hinduism. While calling ourselves 'Hindu' might be a convenient way of talking, the danger lies in going further and trying to develop 'doctrines', 'theologies', 'catechisms' and so on. I wonder how we even managed to keep our traditions alive in light of all these distortions that have taken place over the centuries.

Leela: A good way to appreciate this fact would be to begin by reflecting on how we were taught whatever we were taught. Here is how I grew up. Like most people, I too learnt my tradition from my mother. She hardly went to middle school, never studied Sanskrit, but learnt stories, *shlokas* and *stotras* from her parents. She taught these to me and to my siblings. We went to temples and also subsidized the performance of ceremonies in temples on special occasions. Sometimes a *pundit* would come over to perform a special ceremony, whether it was the *shraaddhas* for my grandparents or sometimes a *havan*. My mother had never read Patanjali or Shankara or anything like that. She read the *Puranas*, and I too was an avid reader of these stories. I copied many verses from these *Puranas* and learnt quite a few of them by heart. Of course, by the time I was in my twenties, I turned into a fire-breathing radical and rejected everything I had grown up with. Today, my life has come around full circle. I have read and studied many writings and commentaries on the ancient texts. But I have come to realize that I learnt much more about the Indian traditions from my mother than I learnt from reading Patanjali or anyone else. Reading the commentaries might allow me to have a cerebral discussion here and there but the question is: where do I stand when compared to my mother? As a practitioner and transmitter of my traditions, I am certainly no better than she was. So, basically, this is what traditions are and this is how we learn them. They are simply sets of practices that our parents pass on to us. These practices are not based on doctrines or justified by reasons and do not embody beliefs that one holds to be true. The notion of practices is wide: from stories through visits to temples, to the performance of rituals. They include the swamis, the festivals, the ashrams and the gurus, and a whole host of other things.

Reeti: I can certainly relate to this. It also accounts for the reason why so many Hindus bemoan the fact that their parents did not teach them anything about Hinduism. When questioned about our 'religion' by people from the West, we feel obliged to come up with some sort of doctrine or belief system. But this is not what we are taught in our homes. In reality, Hindus have never spun out a theology based on the various myths and rituals that they pass along to their children. What they pass along are the *shlokas*, the rituals, the mantras, and of course, the stories. But my only question with reference to this is, since we don't bother with any fixed doctrine or theology, how can we be sure that our traditions are being properly transmitted?

Leela: There is no precise way to transmit a tradition or any preferred manner of doing so. Even though we assume that we have inherited a set of practices from time immemorial, in principle, there is no way of establishing the truth of this belief. Mostly, it is just our grandparents and our parents who transmit these practices. There is no external authority to go by. Changes are bound to have occurred and practices are bound to have adapted themselves to changing times. In fact, traditions live precisely because of their adaptability. But this does not mean that they are either fluid or amorphous. Each one of them is not only distinct from the other but also strives to retain its distinction. To a large extent, the vibrancy of a tradition can be seen by the extent to which it is able to retain its difference from other traditions. Today we don't have any proper understanding to make sense of how traditions can be both very elastic and very dogmatic at the same time.

Arya: Speaking of dogmatism, there are many practices that appear to be rather unjustifiable. How do people decide when to drop a practice or whether to continue it?

Leela: There is no obligation to practice a tradition. If there are good reasons to modify a practice, then, if one is reasonable, one either modifies a practice or abandons it altogether. People don't need to refer to any book or consult any doctrine to determine whether a practice is valid or not. In fact, the more vibrant a tradition the more potential it would have to reject or modify practices as needed. *Moksha* is not denied to you if you don't go to temples or fail to celebrate some festival.

Arya: But many followers of Christianity also just learn various practices and traditions from their parents without imbibing any of the doctrines. In many layers of society you would find little difference between religion and tradition.

Leela: Even though many followers of Christianity learn to participate in their religion from the way they are raised by their parents, they still retain the belief that one needs a reason to continue practicing a religion. And the best reason they have is the truth of their beliefs. This is intrinsic to the nature of their religion which instills the belief that God made the world for a reason, and that their scripture embodies those reasons. One cannot continue to be a Christian if it turns out that Jesus Christ never existed, was never crucified, and the scripture is not a true account.

Because this is how their own religion is, people from such cultures want to know what the Hindus believe in. They think we have our scriptures the way they have theirs. They think that our ways of 'worshipping', which is what they think *puja* is, express our beliefs about how God ought to be worshipped. Of course, they are convinced that we believe in the truth of the *Ramayana* the way they believe in the truth of their stories about Jesus of Nazareth. They think that we believe in the truth of the *Puranic* stories and that we replace our histories and geographies with them. Seriously, have Indians ever believed that seas of liquid butter really existed, and that there were kings thirty feet tall? Our stories cannot be collapsed into some beliefs about the history of humanity without making us appear like complete idiots. But this is exactly what we do when we start talking about our 'own scriptures', our 'own God' and our 'own Ten Commandments' in response to this need for the western world to know what this imaginary entity called Hinduism is. It's about time we realized that we do not need to have a religion thrust upon us; we do not need a 'Hinduism' to find out what we are, or who we are; it's about time we figured out that there are no sublime truths concealed under the loin cloth of Shiva.

Reeti: At least we got that out of the way! But I'm brimming over with further questions and can hardly wait to take them up next.

CHAPTER IV

AND THE REST IS HISTORY

Reeti: Before we embark on anything else, I wanted to say quite emphatically that we Hindus too believe in the truth of our stories. We too feel that our stories actually happened in some particular place and at some point in time. We may not be able to pinpoint the exact date when an event occurred, but we rely on relative dating which goes to show that we care about such things. It's well established, for example, that the events in the *Ramayana* happened before the *Mahabharata*, and that's how most Indians see it.

Leela: As far as relative dating is concerned, the issue is whether the *Ramayana* was composed before the *Mahabharata* and not whether Rama was born before Krishna. Any literature that investigates the truth value of claims made by 'religious texts' is absent in India. This indicates that the question of truth is not the right kind of question to ask with respect to these texts. It makes sense to ask whether the story of the Genesis is true, but it is nonsensical to ask whether the story about one of the incarnations of Vishnu is true. To ask this question about Vishnu is to miss the point of what the story is, namely, a story. It is not a description of the world, nor is it a knowledge claim. To ask whether it is true or false is to assume that it is a knowledge claim, which it is not. Stories serve a different function in the Indian context.

Arya: I see your point, but I guess we can still talk about the truth of our stories as in the context of 'truth in fiction'. Just as we can say, for example, that Sherlock Holmes does not exist but still argue that it is true that he lives on Baker Street. This is a different way of looking at things.

Leela: In our case it is slightly more complex. When we discuss the truth of fictional objects, we know that we are talking about fiction. The fact that we dispute the truth of an event in a story is not the same as an indifference regarding the status of the narrative itself. The *Ramayana* is 'true' though it is not clear what the status of the book is. Perhaps it is fiction perhaps it is not. It is not essential to know whether it is true or not. By contrast, you cannot say with respect to the Bible that the Gospels might or might not be the fictitious invention of four people; or that Jesus might or might not be the Savior. The difference between this and our traditions lies along these lines: to us, the story of Rama does impart knowledge without being a knowledge claim or a truth claim.

Reeti: If you say that it is not important to know whether Rama or Krishna ever lived, what does it mean to be a *bhakta* (devotee) of Rama or Krishna? Doesn't it mean we believe certain things about them? At the very least it means that we display certain attitudes towards them and their stories.

Leela: To *bhakti*, these questions and their answers are utterly immaterial. The *Ramayana* is a way of achieving enlightenment and its efficacy does not depend on such questions or their answers. Intellectual inquiry about these questions will not help you become a *bhakta,* nor will ignorance about these questions prevent you from becoming one. In the Indian intellectual traditions it has never been a topic of significance to discuss whether our stories are true or not. This attitude is true not just of Indians but of Asian culture in general. As a case in point, literally, the first question that the western intellectuals asked when they encountered Buddhism concerned the historical Buddha. By contrast, such questions were not of much interest to the Chinese intellectuals when they encountered Buddhism. So, you see, it is the attitude of a particular culture towards its 'holy books' that generates such questions. The absence of a particular genre of literature in a culture indicates that such a genre is not considered important in that culture. The intellectual constraints of this culture are such that some lines of inquiry do not occur to them, or, where they do, they die out due to lack of intelligibility.

Arya: If truth was not considered important, why then did the Jains proceed to write their own *Ramayana* on the grounds that certain elements in the existing *Ramayana* were false? I remember reading about an ancient Jain scholar who disputed the original account by questioning how monkeys could vanquish powerful *rakshasa* warriors like Ravana; or how noblemen like Ravana could eat flesh and drink blood. If the *Ramayana* is not supposed to be making any truth claims, then why would certain elements of it be considered false by certain people?

Leela: Some Jain authors quite obviously did not agree with the way the world was depicted in the *Valmiki Ramayana*. They did not want to allow *rakshasas* and monkeys to populate their universe of discourse. In conformity with this, they wrote stories that were more plausible to those who shared these views. From this, it does not follow that their stories were historically more accurate or that the *Ramayana* is seen as history. Their stories are also made-up according to their own depiction of the world. When they call the *Valmiki Ramayana* false, they are making claims about logical falsehood. They did not, on the basis of some empirical enquiry, establish that Ravana was a vegetarian or that *rakshasas* were human beings. A mere re-writing of a text does not guarantee that it is true. Therefore, the dissent of the Jain authors merely allows us to note that they disagreed with the way the world was depicted in the *Valmiki Ramayana* and that their claims about falsehoods in *Valmiki* are logically necessary in light of the way they depict the world.

Reeti: But the point is that in the *Ramayana,* Rama existed on earth – he is not merely some abstract concept. Rama is a human being, an *avatar*, who lived in Ayodhya. Thus, to believe Rama exists, means to believe that he existed on earth, in Ayodhya. Please tell me why you keep implying that this conclusion is wrong.

Leela: These things are also related to cultural attitudes. Not everyone means the same thing by 'existence.' If you mean existence as the kind of self-sufficient individuality that people in the western world mean, then a question like "Does Shiva exist?" means one thing. But if all individual existence is merely a temporary and local manifestation of a larger activity, then 'existence' means something more akin to capable-of-being-experienced. If the gods are regarded as forms of the absolute that can be experienced, it is not inconsistent to do *puja* to them while not being concerned about their existence.

I am not denying that people in India and everywhere else in the world hold all kinds of beliefs. The problem is that, as of this time in the twenty-first century, there are no criteria to distinguish between different sorts of beliefs. We cannot distinguish between the structure of the belief that our species is the result of evolution by natural selection and the structure of the belief that tantric dwarfs live on the dark side of the moon.

Arya: That's ridiculous. Most people can tell fact from fantasy and distinguish between scientific theories and fiction.

Leela: I'm talking about the way beliefs are structured in terms of human psychology and not in terms of scientific methodology. There are no scientific criteria available to distinguish between different sorts of beliefs or in the way we treat these beliefs. Believing that our ancestors watch over us is a very different thing from having a factual belief that our dead ancestors are watching over us. We have a long way to go before we can begin to grasp the psychological distinction between beliefs of different types. A Hindu will most likely see no difference between saying "God bless you" and "May the force be with you", whereas an American will probably find it flippant to treat these two blessings in the same way. Since there are no scientific criteria to assess different sorts of beliefs, we do not know how the structure of one belief is different from another belief.

The claims that Christianity, Judaism and Islam make about the world, that is, that God created and governs the universe, that we ought to worship God in order to attain salvation, are claims about the world, which can be characterized as either true or false. Ever since our colonization, the traditional stories from India have been understood as variants of these beliefs. If some people in an Indian village tell you that you have to make an offering of iron to the local goddess otherwise she will harm you, this is seen as the same kind of belief as the claim that Jesus Christ is the son of God. Within this framework we experience the Indian stories as variants of the beliefs in Christianity, Islam, and Judaism. My claim is that this assumption is false. Our stories have a different status. They are a part of a different kind of experience of the world. They have a different place in differently-patterned phenomena.

Arya: Even if this is true in some abstract sort of way, I think that the Hindu rightwing expects us to regard our stories as the factual truth. Remember their jubilation at discovering the *ram setu* – the bridge to Sri Lanka built by Rama's monkey army? There are many such examples that go to show that historical truth is of great importance to Hindus.

Reeti: Really, Arya! You talk as if the Hindu Right holds sway on such matters. You could hardly have failed to notice that their claims are vehemently opposed by the secular set. It is this set of people that wields the real power and goes about determining how Indians should view things.

Leela: In general it is true that one side insists on the historical truth of the Indian legends, while the other side is utterly dismissive of this stance. *Both of these attitudes* are a reflection of our colonial consciousness. They are derived from the same intellectual trend that opposes 'fact' to 'myth' and believes that history must be based on painstaking research and must try and accurately reproduce the past.

Arya: Well, what's the point of having a history at all if it does not accurately reflect the past?

Leela: That depends on why you believe you should study the past at all. These questions are raised in many cultures. Answers to such questions appeal to some idea about what it is to live as human beings, what we aim for in life and why. In other words, we look at the past for the sake of flourishing or being happy in the present. In most groups that have evolved into cultures, there is a sort of an implicit consensus regarding what it means to live a good life. This consensus is as general and as abstract as the question itself. In this sense, each human group has some kind of a story about its past. Indians had their own unique way of recording the past. What Christianity did, however, was to formulate the question about the past within a theological framework. It formulated the question as though the query about the past was inextricably connected with the 'truth' of the story.

Arya: While it is true that in ancient times most cultures only had stories and mythology, I think that seeking the truth about the past is more in line with how most of us think in modern times. From what you just said, I gather that this shift in attitude is related to the growth of Christianity?

Leela: That's right. At the time of its inception, Christianity had to contend not only with the Jews who were skeptical and dismissive of the claims about Jesus, but also with the intellectuals of the Roman Empire who did not buy the claim that some entity called 'God' could create whatever He wanted just by willing it into existence. Caught in this no-win situation, the Christians began to insist more and more vigorously that they were telling the truth. Theirs was not a story or a myth. This was history. The stories that other peoples and nations narrated about their multiple pasts were just that: myths and legends. But the Bible was History. And it was the history, not of this or that nation, but the history of all mankind. If you keep this background in mind, you will be able to make sense of the obsessive need in the West for collecting 'facts' about the past. Everything they claim about their past must not only be true but must also be confirmed by research.

Reeti: I can see that in the West this has to do with the insistence on the truth of the Biblical story. But this is not of any concern to Hindus, so why has it changed our attitude?

Leela: This insistence on truth was a very major development. It brought forth a dramatic change in the cognitive attitude with respect to looking at the past. Consider what happens when you look at actions and events in the world as expressions of God's will. Insofar as God's will is revealed in the world (including in human history), it becomes the task of human beings to study this history to find out what God intends. However, only when we study the past as it actually occurred can we hope to decipher what God intends. An imaginary past is no substitute for an accurate rendering of it because studying false chronicles endangers the very possibility of salvation of the human soul. It was left to St. Augustine to come up with the definitive framework from within which to study the human past. This grand philosophy of history once and for all set the foundation for answering the question: how 'ought' one to study the past? This way of studying the past, or historiography as it is called, has now become one of the legacies of our colonial past.

Reeti: What I don't get is why Indians would want to swap our way of studying the past for a completely different way. It seems silly to insist on the truth of stories.

Leela: Don't forget that the colonial project was also a project of education. This went hand in hand with the missionary project of converting the natives to Christianity. For centuries the missionaries had had great difficulties in getting through to the Hindus. Most Hindus were unimpressed by the Christian approach that revolved around truth, logic, and reasoning when talking about their religion. Gradually the missionaries become convinced that the creation of a proper historical consciousness among the Hindus would have to be one of the preconditions for their conversion to Christianity. This is because historical inquiry provided one of the foundations of the Christian religion by supplying the evidence for the truth of their claims. The natives needed to be educated about the significance of historical assertions and by cultivating their critical faculties. They needed to be taught how to discuss such matters, weigh the evidence, and test the consistency of their views. In this method the missionaries finally found the golden key. Where centuries of efforts in preaching the Bible and talking about the glory of the true God had failed, now, through a secular education and science, they were finally able to get Hindus to think along their lines. This is how we were truly converted, if not necessarily to Christianity, at least to a certain way of thinking. Through a secular education, the British taught us not only how to discuss, but also how to perceive, experience and reflect upon our own traditions.

Reeti: This probably has had its plus and minus points. But from the point of view of our stories, I can't say the effect has been a good one. After all, our stories have been in circulation for millennia and have adequately met the needs of our ancestors as well as our contemporaries. What extra reasons can there possibly be to study the past to find out if things are really true or whether they really happened?

Leela: None at all, as far as I can see. Let's say our stories about the past turn out to be false. So what? What does it matter whether what we believe about our past is true or false as long as it helps us in human flourishing? The only reason to choose truth above falsehood, as far as our stories are concerned, would be if the truth about the past helps us live better as human beings or if the falsehood damages us.

Arya: Well, we could say that we need to know the truth about the past because only as such do we have knowledge about the past. Knowledge is its own justification and does not require any extra reasons to pursue it.

Leela: That may be true, but not in this context. While there's no objection to collecting all sorts of factoids about the past, these don't really have anything to do with 'knowledge', except in a very trivial sense of the word. Historical facts are not capable of explaining anything or establishing a connection between events, no matter what their pretensions towards doing so. Trying to determine the truth of our epics is similar to turning them into repositories of truth in the same way that telephone directories are repositories of truth. Besides, no factoid can ever guarantee the truth-value of historical claims. They can only be surmises and guesses. But they will be pushed across as scientific and historical hypotheses that very soon end up becoming 'facts' about the Indian past. They will acquire the same status as the rest of the claptrap that masquerades as Indological truths.

Reeti: I am beginning to see how this is problematic for us. Indians had their own way of recording the past which is very different from history. They infused their facts with values, took poetic liberties and added lots of human drama to make things interesting. Most of us don't look at our stories for factual information but instead feel an emotional connection with them. If we look at our past only from the colonial framework then we are forced to consider 'truth', 'facts' and 'history' to be more worthwhile than myths and stories. But it's silly to confuse the two and I am a bit bewildered by how we Indians succumbed to this way of thinking, considering that stories are so much more interesting.

Leela: During the Renaissance, when Europe rediscovered ancient Greek culture, it came across many stories about the Greek past, which they called "muthos" or myths. To the Europeans, quite obviously, these myths could not have been true because only their religion possessed the true account of the human past. Since they were obviously false, they wondered why the Greeks composed these myths and what did they 'really' want to say. They came up with many answers, one of them being that myths were disguised historiographies. According to this theory, the poetic imagination transformed historical facts into exaggerated myths. So one needed to interpret these myths to find out what the historical facts were and discard the rest as poetic exaggeration.

By the time Europe encountered India, this was the framework for looking at myths. Most of the multiple theories of myth we have today make the same point: myths require interpretation because poetic imagination has transformed facts into myths. Under colonial rule, the British aggressively pushed their beliefs on to us. They quizzed us about our past in ways we were not used to before. They derided us for believing in the 'truth' of our stories, epics and *Puranas* which they took to be historiographies. Our intellectuals, sadly, succumbed to this attitude because they did not really understand it. It did not occur to Indian intellectuals to study the culture of the colonizers and examine the kinds of questions they were asking. They merely assumed that the attitude of our colonial masters was an exemplification of reason and rationality. They joined in with the British and basically took the only two paths available to them. They either rubbished such stories or tried to show that they were 'true' chronicles of the past. Now you see what I mean when I say that both of these Indian responses – from the right as well as from the left – are derived from the same intellectual trend. They are both based on the western attitude towards history.

Arya: Personally, I've never believed that the *Mahabharata* or the *Ramayana* have anything to do with the truth or history. Neither do most people that I know. Everyone looks forward to the festival season to see the enactments of these epics. It's only the Hindu Right or *Hindutva* that wants to establish all kinds of 'truth' based on these stories.

Reeti: While you're at it, please do not underestimate the destructive powers of the secular Indians. Blissfully unaware of their own profound ignorance, 'secular' historians have always been content to reproduce whatever our colonial masters taught them.

Arya: That may be true, but while the secularists held sway, the damage was somewhat limited. Today, especially in the last few decades, the picture has changed drastically. The tendency now is to insist that our stories about the past are literally our histories and not poetic exaggerations. If you think that the secular Indians are ignorant about western culture, then you've got to admit that the Hindu Right is even more profoundly ignorant of it. Nor does it have any intellectuals of its own. It merely has ideologues. They lack the ability to do any intellectual research, and now they are forced by their own logic to insist that the *Ramayana* is the factual truth.

Leela: I'm afraid that's true. Instead of taking issue with the way the problem had been formulated, the ideologues of the right swallowed the secular articulation of the problem hook, line and sinker. The transformation brought about both by the secular Indians and the rightwing ideologues has been catastrophic. Together they will succeed in doing what centuries of colonialism and missionary activity tried but could not accomplish: destroy Indian culture and its traditions irreplaceably and irrevocably.

Reeti: That would be tragic especially considering that they believe that they are trying to save Indian culture.

Leela: If this continues, we will most certainly cease to relate to our stories as we did before. Our stories have provided us with a deep connection to a collective past. We've rejoiced with Rama, celebrated with Bali, wept with Eklavya, and been touched to the core by the fate of Karna. We get furious at Shakuni, bond with Draupadi, and relate to many of the gods and demons in myriads of ways. This connection is deeper than our connection to our great-grandparents, whom we most likely have never met. As we grow up and learn our geography and science, we try and figure out how there could have been a *treta yuga* when our species is hardly 50,000 years old? How could Bhima really have the strength of 10,000 elephants? How could Dharmaraja walk to the heavens? We turn to our elders with these questions, and their answers, which are really no answers at all, nevertheless satisfy us. And, over a period of time, we stop asking these questions – not because we know the answers but because we somehow learn that these are not the right questions to ask. To grow up as a Hindu is to learn that these stories should be treated differently from claims from our geography and science lessons. We learn that our acceptance of these stories has nothing to do with the truth of these stories. Whether or not some story took place on earth, such a 'fact' is utterly irrelevant.

Reeti: But it is nevertheless exciting to discover that the bridge built by Rama and his monkey army really exists!

Leela: But what happens when people start taking these sorts of claims seriously? In the early phases there is euphoria. Not because we can now say, "ah, after all, everything that the *Ramayana* says is true". But because we feel that our connection to the past has taken on a tangible presence. Suddenly, there is exhilaration! However, this is merely the first phase. What happens in the subsequent phase when this claim is pushed further, as it is invariably going to be? The stories must be stripped off of all their fascinating aspects so that they fit into a socially and historically acceptable framework. On this framework, *rakshasa* and *vanara* cannot be demons and monkeys but merely the names of some tribes in India. Likewise, Krishna and Rama become smalltime tribal leaders; Draupadi becomes a daughter from yet another tribe that practiced polyandry, and so on. Gradually we 'discover' what we knew all along – that it is not possible to train monkeys to build a bridge between India and Sri Lanka.

Reeti: I'd say it's not worth the trade-off. Who would ever want to become a devotee of Rama or Krishna if historiography takes over? How many will go to their temples or even build them?

Leela: That is why it is important to reflect on what we really need – a 'true' factual history or a past that we can relate to and connect with? Most of us in India have accepted the colonial framework. The *Hindutva* people have taken the direct route by saying that our myths are true history. The secular folk have taken the indirect route: they look at myths as stories that require symbolic interpretation. These attempts are no better.

Arya: Again, what do you have against symbolic interpretation? If myths cannot be the literal truth then quite obviously they must be symbolically interpreted. They
could symbolize acts or they could symbolize values. Or
passions, feelings, or even natural forces. The possibilities are endless. I think that this is a much better way of
looking at stories than on insisting on their truth or his-
toricity.

Leela: This, again, has to do with how people in different cultures *treat* stories. Whether a story has something to do
with interpretation or whether it carries a hidden message has nothing to do with the formal structure of a
story but is more of a cultural attitude.

Arya: Of course, you cannot look at the structure of a story and
say what its function is. But how is symbolic interpretation a cultural thing other than the obvious fact that different cultures use different imagery?

Leela: My point is that stories play a different role in different
cultures and I don't believe that stories are treated symbolically in the Indian traditions. To see a moral message embedded in a story is an attitude which is specific
to one culture – western Christian culture. Many Indians
have absorbed this very western notion in multiple ways
and thus raise all kinds of questions. Why perform fu-
nerary rites? What is their significance? What is the
meaning of rituals? What do *mudras* symbolize? And so
on. I'm not sure whether these people themselves are
aware that they're working within the ambit of such a
framework. However, all their objections emerge from
this idea about myths. This is also why many Indians
take umbrage over the interpretations of western scholars. They question whether their stories ever 'intended'
to convey the meanings attributed to them. Or they get
upset if you make a straightforward reference to the rag-
ing sex lives of some of our gods. They would prefer to
see this symbolically interpreted as a 'phenomenon of

the mind', or an interpretation that makes use of the *Vedas* and *Upanishads*, reflecting some 'higher truth'. This goes to show that their attitude towards these stories is very similar to that of our colonial masters and their western counterparts who look at stories as symbols that require interpretation.

Arya: I'm sorry, now you've lost me. Isn't our whole discussion essentially about the fact that the West has come up with strange interpretations of our traditions that we do not relate to? Now you seem to suggest that the interpretations are of less significance than the framework they are embedded in!

Leela: The point I'm trying to make is that in Indian culture stories have nothing to do with interpretation at all. Whether you have interpretation-1, interpretation-2, or interpretation-3, these are all interpretations. It is not the case that the Indian interpretation is somehow better than the western interpretation. We need to abandon this way of looking at stories altogether because I don't believe that this is how stories function in Indian culture.

Reeti: Well, then, how do they function?

Leela: Consider how ubiquitous stories are in India. When children are exposed continuously to stories at all levels of social interaction, these stories end up playing an important role in the process of their socialization and learning to live with others. I think it is reasonable to suggest that in India stories function as units of a learning process.

Arya: But every culture has stories. Why do you think that stories play this type of role only in our culture?

Leela: Because it does not make much sense to speak of units of learning except in the context of a specific learning process. Methods of teaching can teach only to the extent that they dovetail into the process of learning. In

India, the dominant mode of learning is mimetic learning, or learning through imitation, which allows stories to play this role. In cultures where, say, theoretical learning is the dominant mode of learning, stories cannot play the same role. They may entertain and capture your imagination, but they cannot instruct. Stories, in such a culture, become a genre of literature and mostly remain at that level.

Reeti: But what makes stories into units of learning in the first place? Is it the style, the narrative, the structure of the stories, or something else?

Leela: Well, stories are a way of representing the world. Cognitively speaking, they are models of the world in a broad sense of the term. As models, they portray some small part of the world. For instance, let's consider once again our example of a group performing the rain dance or any other ritual. When asked about the significance of their actions, you get to hear a story. Such a story depicts a set of events which includes the performing of the ritual along with some other events. Now, it is not the case that the participants attribute causal efficacy to the performance of such a ritual. That is, the members of the group do not actually believe that their chanting in some specified fashion or the pouring of *ghee* into the fire altar will cause the rains to come. They are not justifying this belief by telling a story.

Reeti: What are they doing then? I realize that they don't quite literally believe that chanting some mantras will cause it to rain, but the stories they tell do tend to depict such things. And they do entertain the hope that the desired result will take place.

Leela: Let's try and understand this by looking at the way in which the members of the group experience the situation. When the ritual is performed and the rains do not come, the group experiences the situation as 'something having gone wrong somewhere'. When the rains do come, it is experienced as 'everything is as it should be'. In any culture, including Indian culture, several hypotheses float around which profess to explain the order of the universe. They account for the pattern that the cosmos exhibits, and provide some explanation of the role of individual actions with respect to sustaining or disrupting that order. Many such explanations have come and gone – why does the sense of order not follow suit? How do such cultures manage to sustain this sense of order in the absence of any knowledge about the pattern? One such mechanism admirably suited for the job is the stories and legends that a culture possesses. Stories preserve patterns without saying what these patterns are. They depict partial aspects of an order without specifying what the order consists of. Performing the ritual and the coming of the rains is a sequence of events described in a story without specifying a relation between them. The experience of 'something having gone wrong somewhere' or that of 'everything is as it should be' is an expression of disturbance or appropriateness to the extent that the story is a model of the situation. So, stories do not explain anything but they do model a set of affairs.

Reeti: I'm still having a hard times seeing what kind of knowledge these stories embody, especially if we rule out symbolic interpretation and moral instruction. How else can they teach us to do anything?

Leela: Stories function as exemplars, and learning through exemplars produces a form of knowledge that can be called action knowledge, or 'knowing how'. In the West, by contrast, the dominant mode of learning is theoretical learning which involves a 'knowing about.' Here, the attitude towards knowledge is textual in nature. Knowledge is seen as something that can be said or explained. Mimetic learning, on the other hand, is sub-intentional learning, that is to say, one learns without being aware that one is learning. Stories do not come with any explicit morals attached nor are they structured as manuals for practical action either.

Reeti: But that's not true! Many Indian stories come with explicit moral instructions. In fact, I recently came across a comic book version of the *Pancha Tantra* where each story had a moral clearly spelled out at the end of it. It had stories such as the one about the sage Yajnavalkya who transforms a mouse into a woman. At the end of the story, there's a bright blue box with the moral "let a mouse be a mouse". Then there was the one about the Brahmin named Mitra Sharma and his goat, to which it was added, "Trust yourself before you trust others". Similarly, there are other stories with their morals clearly spelled out: "Respect your parents" or "Nothing is impossible for a clever person".

Leela: That may well be, and we also have a collection of *subhashitas* or proverbs that revolve around such stories. But, by and large, I suspect that this inclination to simplify stories into clear-cut moral lessons is yet another stance we've picked up because of our western education. If you compare these kinds of moral explanations with your own experience of listening to the stories, perhaps you did not come away with that particular moral explanation. Perhaps you heard the story and just tucked it away somewhere in your mind. This way it allows us to come to different and maybe even better conclusions in a variety of contexts. Instead of conveying the ethical richness of the stories, these moralistic one-liners actually come across as rather impoverished and do a poor job of conveying our cultural attitudes towards life.

Reeti: Well then, we're back to square one. If stories can teach, and if, according to you, their primary job is not to pass along morals, what exactly are they doing?

Leela: Within this process of learning, stories serve as action heuristics in terms of creating some capacity in a person. They are not meant to serve as facts that are subject to interpretation or that can be characterized as true or false. So you see, it is a completely different way of looking at stories where interpretation plays no role whatsoever. To treat stories as something that require interpretation is to look at them as textual entities. In that case, learning from them becomes purely a matter of drawing analogies or justifying practices by referring to the story.

Reeti: What exactly are action heuristics?

Leela: A heuristic is a rule of thumb that helps with problem-solving, or helps in learning and discovery through trial and error. In exactly the same way that an idea or a theory generates new ideas, an action is capable of generating new actions. This is what I mean by 'action knowledge' which is distinct from theoretical knowledge. It is not as if you read or hear a specific instruction and this gives you some ideas for a future action. But rather, through mimesis or exemplary learning, actions generate new actions that you could not do before. And all of this occurs sub-intentionally; we learn without being aware that we are learning. Even though exemplars are context-bound, they can be generative in multiple contexts. In this sense, mimesis is creative and dynamic.

In western culture, the dominant approach is to treat whatever life brings your way as some sort of a decision-making problem. This is not the case with mimetic learning. Our difficulties do not revolve around making choices between alternatives. Rather, acquiring the ability to execute a new action is the same as knowing what to do. Problems regarding action knowledge are not decision problems; they are learning problems. Of course it is possible to describe them as decision problems if necessary, but their basic function is not that.

Reeti: Wait, I have a problem with this. You say that mimetic learning means learning through imitation. Quite obviously we're meant to imitate good behavior. But considering that mimetic learning is sub-intentional, what's to prevent us from learning to imitate bad behavior?

Leela: Once again, you're thinking in terms of the framework we've inherited from the West. Unlike in the West, there are no normative rules in Indian thinking. Right and wrong has everything to do with context and nothing to do with some ethical principle that is supposed to be applicable at all times to all people. Action heuristics are not subject to truth claims. As embodied in the stories, they are not even restricted by requirements of consistency and coherence. Rather, their efficacy is relative to how well they succeed in generating appropriate actions, both internally as modes of reflection and externally as attitudes towards oneself and others.

Arya: I think I can see why stories would be the perfect vehicle to transport attitudes and inclinations without actually spelling them out. This can only happen when we learn without being aware that we are being taught.

Leela: Exactly. Besides, action knowledge must not be seen as knowledge about actions, but something that generates an ability to execute new actions. This ability to learn new actions is indifferent to the presence or absence of goals. One of the fundamental beliefs in the western world is that action is goal-oriented, and that this constitutes the basic property of actions. Just the opposite is true. Intrinsically, human action is goal-less. Quite obviously this does not prevent one from finding a goal for an action. But mimesis, as sub-intentional learning, has nothing to do with the presence of goals, whether good or bad.

Of course this is hard to believe now if you consider the way Indian parents are bent on fashioning a brand of

Hinduism based on nineteenth-century Victorian prudery. They're busy peddling this ironed-out, one-dimensional, puritanical, neo-Vedantic strain of Hinduism to their kids without realizing that it is actually doing them incalculable harm. It is this attitude that makes them feel embarrassed about being Hindus when confronted with the full-blooded Indian traditions. How do you 'explain' that our *devas* are avid adulterers or that our *apsaras* are nothing but prostitutes in the court of Indra? What kind of a symbolic explanation can you give for Krishna and his *rasa lila* with 16,000 women at a time? How can you explain *kama*, one of our basic *purush arthas*, which is acceptable as a legitimate goal of human striving? What will these kids do, when they discover that this antiseptic 'Hinduism' they are being taught is belied by the stories from our own traditions which say all of the above and ever so graphically?

Reeti: Whoa, put your brakes on! I understand your larger point but some of your statements are way off the mark. You could say that our traditions had a humane attitude towards prostitution, but to say that *apsaras* are no more than prostitutes is an extreme statement. *Apsaras* were highly respected for their knowledge of poetry, music, dance and other artistic disciplines. They were sophisticated and intelligent. Similarly, *kama* as a *purusha artha* covers a broad range that includes the arts and anything that pleases the senses. Sexual pleasure and romantic love constitute only a part of it. Our traditions have a rich legacy of literature that uses allegories to talk about life and to instill love and respect for human beings and animals.

Leela: The question is not whether our stories instill any of these feelings. The problem is that we have come to accept a normative way of looking at stories and to extract some alleged Hindu beliefs out of them. This is how we end up facing silly questions like "Why do Hindus worship cows"? or "Why do Hindus worship the toe of the

Shankaracharya?" You may sense that there's something wrong with such questions, that they raise a pseudo-problem, but you are not able to show how they do so. You may sense that the question restricts your thinking about Indian ethics instead of allowing for an explanation. You may even express your irritation. But in the end all you can do is either shrug your shoulders or give a silly answer like "Indians worship the toe of the Shankaracharya because reverence for the guru is the most important thing in their culture." Once again, this reveals the bizarre situation we are in today. Such questions presuppose a Christian theological framework and then look for descriptions of the Indian traditions through this framework. The same framework constrains the answers we can give. We are forced to stay within this framework no matter what answers we come up with.

Reeti: I agree that we have to face some really silly questions. I never know what to say when people ask me why we worship cows or don't eat beef. But what does this have to do with any theological framework?

Leela: It has to do with the idea that ties practices to beliefs. Once we get inside this framework, we are compelled to come up with a deep reason for the fact that most Hindus don't eat beef. In reality, it cannot be that Hindus 'worship' cows in particular because Hindus hold the same attitude towards many other animals as well. Besides, you only have to look at the sorry state of the cows in India to realize that they're not exactly being worshipped. The truth is more along the lines that most Hindus simply don't see cows as food. It's the same as asking Americans why they don't eat dogs. Of course, we can always keep pestering them to provide a deep reason for this fact, and, being Americans, they'll probably oblige by coming up with a 'deep' reason or two, but the answer is really quite simple.

Reeti: Can it really be that simple? I often feel there's something unconvincing about deep reasons, but then I
thought that that was just me.

Leela: We often find ourselves in such predicaments during in-
ter-cultural dialogs. The West interprets the practices or
stories of Hindus in a particular way and puts forward
their interpretation as an 'explanation' of the Hindu traditions. The Hindu disagrees, feels violated, and wants
to defend their traditions. The fact is that when you enter
into a dialog, you are compelled by the rules of rational
dialog to express your disagreement in terms of reasons.
If you don't agree with their set of reasons, you are expected to offer an alternative set of reasons. However,
in this way, the dialog is skewed in favor of the West,
because it compels the Hindu to accept the framework
through which the West approaches the Indian traditions, that is, through the framework of intentional psychology (based on beliefs, reasons and desires). This
forces Hindus to come up with some kind of an explanation of their tradition. But, as we already discussed,
traditional practices do not require an explanation. Unless, that is, you belong to a culture that thinks practices
are tied to beliefs, and that actions are performed in accordance with reasons.

The encounter between western culture and Hindu culture has compelled educated Hindus to enter into the
framework of intentional psychology. Consequently,
they now feel they have to give all kinds of 'rational explanations' for their traditions, stories and practices. So
they come up with absurd claims like Krishna's sixteen
thousand *gopis* are an allegorical representation of the
endings of the nervous system, or that *kumkum* is used
because it has a certain effect on the mind, or that
Vishnu's *avatars* are a symbolic representation of evolutionary biology, and so on and so forth. Notice that
these explanations often take the form of symbolic or
allegorical interpretations of the stories. Also notice that

such explanations, even when given by Hindus, trivialize and distort the Indian traditions. After all, should people stop using *kumkum* when science comes along and proves that the explanation about the nervous system is utter nonsense? Should you begin to feel deeply ashamed if it turns out that Krishna's *gopis* cannot really be about any allegorical representation? This is the contemporary situation in which our dialogs on Shiva and his phallus take place.

If you look at stories as something that require interpretation, then your claims play the same role as the western claims with respect to the Indian myths. So the feeling that your experience has been trivialized and violated becomes even stronger. Crucially, it is *you* who have trivialized and distorted your own experience of the Indian traditions by accepting the framework of intentional psychology. You have internalized that framework to such an extent that it has become an automatic mode of understanding the nature of the Indian traditions. Your protests can be seen as an attempt to break free of the constraints of this framework. However, to break free of these constraints we first need to study the culture that has projected this way of thinking on to us. Only then can we free ourselves from the grip of the cognitive structure that compels us to see stories and practices as objects of interpretative, allegorical or symbolic explanation.

Arya: Whew! For whatever it is worth, I think that the West has undergone a huge paradigm shift in the last half century or so. Although many people regard the Bible to be a true account, there is nevertheless a shift in attitude away from looking at it as the literal truth. With the increasing impact of science this is going to become more and more significant.

Leela: It's true that it is becoming increasingly more popular to look at the Bible in its entirety as a series of stories, and the Greek distinction between *mythos* and *logos* has come under criticism. But this trend is not comparable to the stance in the Indian case. Whatever the intellectual trend in Biblical scholarship, we must not forget that these are responses to the historical problems posed by the textual analysis of the Bible. Even where the Gospel is seen as a story, it becomes an object of investigation as a text. Only as a text can the Bible provide knowledge. Such an attitude dovetails into the point made earlier that knowledge is primarily textual in nature in the West. Consequently, even the narrative trend requires knowledge of the text. Plus, it looks at the text of the Bible as a story without, however, being able to look at stories in other ways. Stories are treated as knowledge-claims of some kind, whether moral, ethical or factual.

Arya: No doubt there is a cultural difference in attitude, but I think that the secular worldview is slowly replacing the religious mindset all over the world. I think that the religious outlook will be increasingly marginalized in the not-too-distant future.

Leela: In that case, you will be hugely disappointed to learn that the secular worldview is not as free of religious constraints as you might like to believe. A mere change in vocabulary does not indicate a change in our cognitive paradigm. Our views about religion or human nature are not isolated beliefs that we can easily get rid of. We have to gradually replace a larger conceptual framework that structures our experience with an alternative framework that will structure our experience in a different way. As things stand now, this shift has not taken place. The distinction between the religious and the secular that you speak of is *drawn by religion* and is *within* religion. We might call it secular, but it is still a religious world.

Arya: I have no idea what you're talking about, but I'm definitely intrigued. This sounds like something we can spend a great deal of time talking about. Perhaps we should start afresh tomorrow?

CHAPTER V

THE DEVIL IN THE DETAILS

Arya: Okay, you have some serious explaining to do. I understand that when you say 'religion' you essentially mean Christianity, Judaism and Islam, that is to say those religions that regard the universe to be something intelligible, a manifestation of God's will, and so on. The indigenous Indian traditions do not fit into this framework so I will try and keep this distinction in mind when I use the word 'religion' from now on. But my burning question right now is this: what did you mean when you said that the distinction between the religious and the secular is drawn by religion and is within religion? I cannot even begin to make sense of what you mean.

Leela: Well, you could begin by noting that religion is some kind of a system that keeps spreading and reproducing itself. There are many dynamics that allow religion to spread, such as worship, proselytization, conversion, or territorial expansion. Mostly, when people talk about the expansion of religion, this is all that they mean. The opposite processes are called the processes of secularization. When, for instance, religion starts losing out, wins fewer converts, or say, when religion begins to withdraw from public life, or fails to spread. This withdrawal of religion from spheres where it was explicitly present before is said to be a sign of the spread of secularization.

Now, the hypothesis I'm developing acknowledges all of these different dynamics. However, what I would like to suggest is that secularization is not a sign of the withdrawal of religion but is actually one of the ways in which religion *expands*. Secularization is a way in which religion, in fact, universalizes itself. It is the way in which Christianity, for instance, spreads by generalizing its religious ideas in a non-religious fashion, or by forming 'secular' institutions that embody religious ideas. On this view, it makes little difference if you say that you are an atheist or ignorant about religion in every way. The fact of the matter is that your worldview is nevertheless structured by a religious framework that is disguised in secular terminology.

Arya: But you know very well that I'm a blue-blooded atheist and a proud believer in secularism. Other than trying to tolerate the religious world, I have nothing to do with religion. I cannot imagine what dynamic of religion you have conjured up that puts both the religious and the secular in the same camp.

Leela: Remember, the world of religion includes everything; it is the world of God's will and the world of his creation. That means it necessarily includes everything, including the secular world. It is not a question of some theologian drawing a distinction between the spiritual and the temporal, but about the coming-into-being of two worlds: the world of religion and the world of human beings. The world of human beings might include such things as the law, the state, cemeteries, child-rearing practices, computer engineers, and the building of cities. But it has been designated as the secular world by the religious world. In other words, the secular world is brought forth by the religious world as a *secularized religious* world.

Reeti: I'm sorry, I am totally lost. I'm trying to take this seriously and have no doubt that there's a point in there somewhere. Please help me see it a bit more clearly.

Leela: Okay, let's draw upon our pagan friends from Rome once again to see if we can get a better grip on this. The entire pagan world was what we today would describe as a secular world, which is to say, consisting of man-made institutions and traditions. Christianity was born and began to expand in this secular pagan milieu. As it grew, it began to make a distinction between the religious and the secular – between the world relating to God and the world relating to human beings. This distinction did not exist before the Christians began to make it, because for the Romans everything was secular.

Reeti: But if the Roman world was littered with gods and goddesses how can it have been a secular world? Is this because, on your hypothesis, the Roman traditions were not religions in the sense that Judaism, Christianity and Islam are religions?

Leela: That's one aspect of it but not the particularly relevant one in the present context. The point I'm trying to get across is that the pagan world was the *totality* of all pagan practices. The Romans did not divide the world into separate spheres such as religious or civic or secular. It's Christianity that first drew this distinction in viewing certain institutions such as the monastery or the church as institutions representing God's will on earth, rather than as secular human organizations. Naturally it confronted a problem when it began to expand within the pagan world. From all the practices in pagan society, it needed to determine which were truly pagan practices and which merely those performed by the pagans. Remember, the devil played a big role in this religion and it was crucial for them to determine which practices constituted devil worship and which were legitimately civic. Thus began the separation of social practices into distinct and separate realms. There were practices that reflected true religion and worship, those that were secular (or civic), and those that were prohibited, that is, they constituted idolatry or false religion.

Reeti: What practices are we talking about in general?

Leela: Almost everything came under their scrutiny. Practices like honoring a martyr on his feast day by getting drunk; attending circus games and spectacles; banquets, giving presents, holding races and games were some of the practices that came under consideration. Some of the church fathers found these to be an expression of devil worship; Augustine found them more neutral. Some Christians thought that celebrating the New Year was not wrong; some others attacked it virulently. What one ate, how one dressed, what jewelry one wore, these too were matters for theological reflection. As Christianity expanded within the pagan world, the pagans too began to have this distinction between the religious world and the secular world thrust upon them. And as Christianity gained political recognition and economic power, the pagan world had to be absorbed into the Christian scheme. Thus, by making a distinction between the sacred and the secular, Christianity brought about a contraction of the secular pagan world, which prior to this had been totally secular. Now the pagan world was also divided into the sacred and the secular.

Reeti: You know, in a way I can immediately relate to what you just said. Since we're the pagans now, if we look at it from the Indian context, it becomes quite easy to see. Even though we city-bred folk have learned to speak in terms set forth by our colonizers, the vast majority of Indians tend not to separate the world into different spheres. For instance, I recently attended a huge celebration in a village in Andhra for the death anniversary of a great *yogi*. There were all kinds of people and activities: *sadhus*, swamis, magicians, astrologers, dice games, drums, dancers, singers, strip-dancing transvestites, processions, chanting, *pujas*, beggars, alcohol, rooster fights, and peddlers of each and every stripe. Everybody had converged on this village for the event, and it's easy to see that there is no sharp divide between the religious and the secular here, even if some of us have learned to characterize such things as 'religious' events. Where the English-speaking Indians see hypocrisy, superstition and a crossing of boundaries, the villagers don't seem to have the same experience at all.

Leela: Exactly. By dividing and segregating some practices as religious, Christianity defined the boundaries of what qualified as religious and what qualified as secular. In this way, it is a Christian-secular world that came into being as generated by a Christian-religious world. That is why this secular world of ours is in the grips of a religious world. The early Christians experienced the Roman world as one dominated by false religion which permeated all walks of life. Our contemporary western world experiences other cultures in exactly the same way. They don't call it false religion, but they see it as religion nonetheless. That is why you often find statements in books about how all Asian thought is religiously conditioned. But only if you insist on utilizing a Christian theological framework does it appear to be this way.

Arya: This is very interesting but I think we may have digressed a little. I thought we were trying to understand how the secular world is a means for the expansion of religion. What you just said shows how the world has been divided into two spheres. This does not explain how religion universalizes itself.

Leela: As we already discussed, religion has to be couched in some or the other doctrine. Universalization of religion merely implies that the structure built by these doctrines becomes so well-entrenched that even when their specific theology fades into the background this cognitive structure stays in place. It is as though the logical form of religion is able to stay intact by getting rid of its semantic content. Thus, both at the level of folk psychology and in the scholarly consensus in western academia, the background assumptions of Christian doctrine are accepted even while its specific teachings may be rejected. So it's not as if any fixed teachings are spread in

society, but rather certain attitudes and orientations towards life and the world in general.

Reeti: What kinds of attitudes are we talking about?

Leela: Religion places certain constraints on the intellectual
and practical energies of religious cultures; it develops
a sense of relevance or importance; people from religious cultures begin to look at human lives, actions, or
historical events as carriers of meaning, intention and
purpose; they conceive of all cultural ethics as bodies of
norms; they approach society as a system constituted by
a legal framework; they experience natural phenomena
as linked to each other by an underlying order, and so
on. Thus, even though the core theology is no longer
present, the empirical possibilities or impossibilities that
it specifies continue to lurk as background constants that
cannot be challenged. For example, such constraints do
not allow for negative answers to ideas such as whether
there is a God, or whether all cultures have religion.

Arya: I think you are drastically overstating the relevance of
God and religion. In fact, it is almost irrelevant at this
point in our history when half the world does not even
believe in God. I realize that this may be less true in the
U.S., but it certainly is the case in Europe.

Leela: I see I'm having difficulty getting my point across once
again. The secular world is the *same* as the religious
world, except for a change in vocabulary. It is a form of
religion in a new *avatar*. Even if you take God out of
the picture, his shadow still lurks in all sorts of ways.
The specific theology, along with its whole kit and ca-
boodle, has faded into the background so it does not
look like religion any more. However, since its cognitive structure has stayed in place, it is no different from
religion (although in secularized garb). That is why I
view it as an expansion of religion because many secular
themes stem from explicitly theological ideas. A theo-

logical question does not cease to be theological just because those who study it do not know much about God or theology. The very fact that such questions make sense at all and do not appear nonsensical is proof of the fact that the questioner remains within the ambit of a religious framework.

Arya: This is again way too abstract for me to fully grasp. If things are really as you claim, you should be able to come up with some fairly concrete examples to illustrate your point.

Leela: Actually, this process has been going on for a long, long time, in fact, since the very inception of Christianity. In general, people believe that the Enlightenment, which is also called the Age of Reason, culminated in bringing about a secular world. The Enlightenment thinkers are supposed to have successfully fought against the dominance that religion had exercised over social, political, and economic life. With the triumph of the Enlightenment, or so goes the standard text book story, people began to look to Reason, instead of, say, the Church in all matters social, civic, or political.

Arya: You can count me in. I stand on the shoulders of these great Enlightenment thinkers and am a firm believer in the role of reason in social life; I recognize the value of human rights, equality, fraternity, and all the rest of it. We owe these thinkers a great deal.

Leela: As I said, this is the standard text book story. The problem with this story is simply this: the Enlightenment thinkers built their reputation as opponents of religion by peddling ideas from Protestant Christianity as though they were *neutral* and *rational*. If you keep this in mind and then take a close look at the social sciences, you will find plenty of evidence for this. The intellectual constraints imposed by religion are such that theory-formation in the social sciences often takes the form of merely filling in empty theological constants in the background while interpreting some variables in the foreground. Funnily enough, God has become one of the empty constants with the ever-increasing popularity of atheism and can now take the form of 'nature,' 'evolution,' 'humanity,' or 'natural law'. But the attitude and orientation towards whatever replaces God still remains religious.

Reeti: I'm not sure I get it. If by attitude and orientation you are referring to things like the deep-seated sense that there is an underlying order behind natural phenomena, then that's actually a very good thing considering that it resulted in giving us the natural sciences.

Leela: I am not trying to point out if it is a good thing or a bad thing. We need to understand it first. Yes, we already talked about how some of the concept clusters generated by religion led to the development of the natural sciences in the West. This is a result of the secularization of a cluster of theological ideas about the natural world. For instance, medieval monks were the first naturalists who named, described, and classified all kinds of species of animals and plants, simply because this was a way of worshiping God. Honoring, describing, and celebrating the incredible diversity in His Creation was a way to express one's surrender to His will. This is one of the most fascinating aspects of the Christian religion because it generated an attitude that has led to some wonderful discoveries in the natural sciences. Unfortunately, the same cannot be said for its effect on the social sciences. These sadly masquerade as science but, if anything, they prevent the emergence of knowledge about human beings and their cultures and societies.

Arya: Now you've piqued my interest. I can barely curb my disdain for the social sciences. The natural sciences have progressed beyond all imagination while the social sciences remain stagnant and never cease to sound borderline ridiculous. Despite the science of economics, psychology, or political theory, there's still as much poverty in the world, people are just as unhappy as ever, and there's no sign of world peace. You'd think that for all their theorizing they'd have at least made a dent somewhere. But why this difference if they both originate from the same source of inspiration?

Leela: It's because the theories and ideas in the natural sciences carry the criteria for testing and evaluating these ideas within the theories themselves. They do not depend on background assumptions. For instance, it is irrelevant to Einstein's theories whether or not he believed that God plays dice with the universe. Such ideas may provide a form of inspiration but they are not a part of the theory nor do they have any consequences on the theory. The same is not true of the social sciences. These are squarely based on ideas derived from Christian theology. Even though both the natural sciences and the social sciences are the result of religion, they are so in hugely different ways. The natural sciences are a result of the development of a configuration of learning in western culture while the social sciences are the result of the secularization of Christian ideas.

Arya: Can we talk about the secularization of religious ideas some more? While I am totally on board with the idea that the social sciences are worthless, I don't see how it relates to religion. Except perhaps as a form of imperialism or racism. The field of Indology alone is enough to testify to this.

Leela: I have been reflecting on these matters deeply, seriously, and systematically for some time now. To say that this is racist is not adequate because it ends up transforming *all* writers who provide such descriptions into racists or Orientalists. This simply cannot be the case. Moreover, these writers include not just western scholars but most Indian ones as well. So there has to be some other dynamic involved that makes the scholarship come out as being racist.

Arya: I agree that buzz-words like 'racist' don't really explain anything. We need to understand why these attitudes persist, reproduce themselves and infect the Indians. It would be a fun exercise to reverse the gaze and do a sort of a "Westology".

Leela: In a way, you could say we need to do to the West what it has done to the rest of the world, that is, study it anthropologically. But you must realize that the social sciences use the same methods to analyze the West as they do the rest of the world. If we do what you suggest, we would simply reproduce what generations of thinkers from the West have already said about the West. Our problems do not begin or end in religious studies or Indology. They are deeper. Much, much deeper. To tackle them simply as a matter of racism would be to compound tragedy with conceptual blunder. It would prevent us from understanding the problem for what it is: a phenomenon that is *typical of western culture*. The only way I have been able to account for this state of affairs is by suggesting that the social sciences themselves are suspect. The social sciences, or the tools used by the western world to study cultures, are actually secularized versions of Christian theologies.

Arya: That's a tall claim and one that you have been repeatedly making in the last few minutes. Since you did say you've been thinking about these matters deeply, seriously, and systematically, I'll reserve my comments for now. But go on.

Leela: Over the last two thousand years, Christianity has worked out immensely sophisticated notions of Man, Society, and so on. These notions have become a part of our daily language, whether you speak English, French, German, Italian, or any other European language. These Christian ideas about man and his psychology, society and culture, have become the *presuppositions* for what we call the social sciences and the humanities today. This is what I mean by the secularization of Christianity.

These ideas are so deep and so pervasive within western culture that they set limits to western imagination itself. It is simply not possible for this culture to imagine that other ways of thinking and going about in the world are possible. One of the consequences of looking at things from this perspective is that all other cultures end up becoming pale and erring variants of western culture. In exactly the same way that all other cultures supposedly have some form of religion, which naturally is a pale and erring variant of Christianity.

Reeti: Can we take a break from religion for a bit? If you're talking about the social sciences in general, then let's talk about psychology, or political science, or economics. Have ideas from theology found their way into these sciences as well?

Leela: How could they not have if my claim is that the social sciences are saturated with theology? Since you mention psychology, let's begin with that. One of the central notions in psychology, the idea of the 'person' or 'self' is a secularization of the Christian notion of 'soul'. This theological idea has more or less been translated to mean our 'individual personalities' and now masquerades as a scientific idea in disciplines such as developmental psychology and clinical psychology.

Arya: I have only a fuzzy notion of what the soul is supposed to be, but let's not even go there. What is the idea of the 'self' in the social sciences, or rather in western culture?

Leela: Many conceptions of the self have been worked out, but I believe that it is possible to pick out one dominant conception that can basically be called *the* western model of the self. Similarly, the East too has multiple ideas of the self but we could distill one dominant notion that could be called *the* eastern notion of the self. That is to say, the notions of the self as conceptualized by the intellectual traditions both in the East and the West are also present in the folk psychologies of these two cultures. So, to keep it simple, we can address this topic from the level of folk psychology.

The basic conception of the 'self' in western culture is that in each human being there is an inner core which is separate and different from everything else. Human beings are seen as biological organisms endowed with a self. Consequently, unlike in the East, human beings do not build a self but create an identity for the self. This already-existing self acquires the identity which the human organism builds for it. This self is something that can grow and actualize itself, that is, it can realize its potential or fail to do so. Such a self is aware of itself as a self, or has self-consciousness. When one speaks of "finding oneself" it means that one should look inside oneself to get in touch with an inner self. Again, unlike in the East, this inner self is not related to actions but there is the conviction that it is somehow different from the actions one performs. I realize that when I express it explicitly in this fashion, you may not be willing to accept the suggestion that such a concept of the self is *the* western conception of the self. But this becomes apparent when you consider that certain western notions in the legal and ethical domain are simply incomprehensible without precisely such a concept of the self. For instance, such a conceptualization makes it *plausible* in western culture to plead temporary insanity to make a case that your actions came from somewhere that was not your real self.

Arya: Well, if you put it that way, it does seem plausible. But the funny thing is that I can relate to most of what you say about the notion of the self and I'm not from the West. I too feel there is an inner self inside me. The only thing that I don't relate to is the idea that a person's actions can be separated from who they are.

Leela: This goes to the crux of the matter when looking at the self from the eastern perspective. In the East, the idea of the self is actually an identity relation between actions and persons. There is no distinction made between an agent that acts and the actions that the agent performs. The self is constituted by the actions that it performs, or to state it even more starkly, an agent or self is the actions performed and nothing more.

Arya: This is a bit extreme. Surely I am more than my actions? To be honest, I have not really thought much about these things but I'm having trouble relating to this.

Leela: Let's look at an example to illustrate this idea. Suppose you were to ask someone to tell you what person X is like. Perhaps their response would be to say that "she is a kind and loving person". Or you would be told something along the lines that "she always makes sure everyone else in the family has eaten before she eats." Notice that in the second instance we are not speaking about the disposition of the person but of her actions. This, I suggest, is a very typical way of answering such questions in India. They appear not to be answering the question at all but in fact they do, and they do so in action terms.

Arya: But one of the attributes of a kind and loving person could well be that they would eat only after everyone else in the family has had their meal. There's not much of a difference between looking at this in terms of their disposition or in terms of their actions.

Leela: That may be so, but there's more to it. The nature and the character of the actions that person X performs depends very much upon person Y. There is a relational construction of the self in the sense that X constructs Y's self and Y constructs X's self. Person Y is required to make X's actions be seen as some specific type of action. In other words, the self of X crucially depends upon continuously being recognized as this type of self by Y. For instance, you can be a son, a mother, a friend, or an employee only to the extent that you are recognized as such by the person you are relating to. And you can only be recognized as such when you perform those actions which are appropriate to the 'station' of being a son, a mother, a friend, or an employee. In India, the self is a meaningless bundle of actions created by human beings. The psychological identity of such a self comes from its actions and from its construction of the 'other'. A human being who builds such a self is conscious, to be sure, but lacks that self-consciousness which is supposed to typify human beings.

Reeti: I guess this would be one explanation for the curious fact that in India there are so many names for different types of relationships. It's still very much a custom not to call people by their names but to just address them according to the relationship you have with them. This goes beyond family relationships and extends even to professional relationships. Also, I've noticed that it's more common in the West to say things like "He loves me for myself", or "This is who I am", as if who you are has nothing to do with the person you are relating to. As if that proverbial tree falling in that forest always makes a crashing sound even when there's no-one around to hear it....

Leela: It's true that the relational aspect of the self is very much marginalized in the West. Instead, human beings are conceptualized as having selves whose nature it is to be unique. A human being builds a psychological identity for such a self, which is what makes such a being unique. Self-knowledge in western culture amounts to self-representation. It's a mixture of things like memories, ideas, values, race, gender, all rolled up and glued together by emotions. As long as this picture is not subjected to too many shocks, a person comes to recognize this as their identity. The actions performed by such a self are made intelligible by explaining them in terms of intentions or belief-states. It becomes possible to give an intentional account of human actions because the self supposedly has these beliefs, desires and fears and for this reason performs such and such action. These are the kinds of explanations of human behavior given by the various theories of intentional psychology.

Arya: But what other type of account can you give for human actions other than that they are intentional? Even as we speak, I am brimming with hopes, desires, ambitions, and fears which I consider to be the reasons for which I do what I do. Otherwise, why bother getting out of bed in the morning?

Leela: Believe me you would get out of bed in the morning regardless of your ambition or lack thereof. That's what a human being does – it acts. Just as the mind thinks, the body acts. In the Asian traditions, human beings are seen more as the *bearers of a dynamic* than as agents. The intentionality of human actions is seen as an illusion. It is not the case that we are full of multiple desires, fears and ambitions. Our traditions speak of such things in the singular. They tell us that what we have is, say, Desire. The nature of Desire is such that it can attach itself to anything. It could be about a Barbie doll, a fancy car, chocolate cake, or alcohol. There are not multiple desires, but one and the same entity called Desire that can attach itself to anything it feels like. Desire has no intrinsic goal; it is limitless and nothing can satisfy it. Our inability to satisfy Desire has to do with the very nature of Desire itself. That is why our traditions tell us that it is of no use looking at the 'aboutness' of such intentional states. What we need to do is to understand Desire itself, and learn to live with it in the best possible way. Our traditions have worked out many ways of coping with such things, comprising of paths that range from the ascetic to the indulgent. The common element in all of them is the insight that the way to understand Desire is through knowledge of the Self.

Reeti: So, knowledge of these so-called intentional states is something like a stepping stone? I mean, when we begin our introspection, do we first have to deal with all of these things such as desire, anger, fear, before reaching the Self?

Leela: I don't think introspection is something that would help in this context. Again, this way of thinking is something we've borrowed from the West, without much reflection. Let me illustrate the difficulty with introspection by using my own example. As you know, I have a very short fuse and lose my temper rather quickly. No amount of self-admonition, remorse, advice, or self-help manuals have helped. Most of us are all too familiar with the endless loop these kinds of problems generate and the burden they place on us. I am unhappy with the way I am and punish myself for it. I genuinely wish I would change, but the beast simply refuses to budge. Why? There are two kinds of problems here – one about my short temper and the other generated by the way I think about myself. In fact, most of the problems that make life so painful are generated by the way I think about myself and not by my temper. This familiar way of thinking about oneself is introspection.

I would suggest that the biggest obstacle to self-change is this process of introspection and not the way a person is. This process of introspection presupposes something about human psychology that is remarkable to say the least. It tells me that this short temper of mine expresses something unique about me and tells me (and the world at large) what kind of a creature I am. Consequently, if I want to change, I have to transform this short temper and all such unique qualities that I possess. If things like my temper are my unique properties, then what are the properties that I share in common with my fellow human beings? I share the biological foundation such as genes, cells, body and brain. That means to say, this biological inheritance forms the foundation of who I am, and above this foundation, a structure gets built. This structure expresses my unique nature and my individual psychology. From this point of view, this structure is what we are, so that changing ourselves requires intro-spection and involves delving into this structure. The lower we go in this structure, the more we share with other human beings. The higher we go, the more unique we are. Disciplines like depth psychology, psychoanalysis, or introspection relate the structure to some 'layer' that is common either across a small group of people, say, those who suffered child abuse, or across a bigger layer, say, women. Whatever the explanation they come up with, the point is this: this structure is who we are and any analysis can only relate some layers of this structure to other layers from the same structure. This is the image behind the process of introspection we are so familiar with. But notice that the apex of this structure is an expression of my unique nature. This means that the problem is with the structure itself, or in the way I am uniquely 'me'. In short, my problem is precisely with what I take to be my uniqueness! Hopefully, you can now understand why introspection leads to endless loops and that the problem lies not in how we are but with how we think about ourselves.

Arya: But what other ways are there to think about ourselves? Can we think about ourselves without introspection?

Leela: Yes, we can, even though we have now adopted the western way of looking at things so our Indian practices are not so readily available. But they still dominate parts of village life and are a testament to the availability of alternate ways of going about in the world. Suppose that I was born in a village somewhere in the interior of Karnataka, and let's suppose too that I had the same short fuse. How would my social circle have looked at it and taught me to go about with it? After umpteen attempts to help me control my temper, my parents would have simply given up on me. But, in the course of this process, and as a result of their failure, they would have also perhaps given me a nickname. Something along the lines of Durvasa or Rudra, or Kali, that reflects a quick temper. In any case, the entire community would have known about this idiosyncrasy. As I got socialized, I would also learn that 'this is how I am' and that there is little I can do about it. In short, both my social circle and I would have learnt to accept it as an idiosyncrasy of mine. I would learn to live with it without being obsessed about it. I would not subject myself to endless self-recrimination about the fact that I lose my temper. My society and my culture would teach me that the structure that gets built on the foundation consists of such idiosyncrasies and is not worth fretting about. Everyone is, in this sense, idiosyncratic and with me it happens to be my short temper.

Notice the difference in this process. What, in the West, is seen as the uniqueness of a person and that which constitutes the core of one's being and requires introspection, is merely seen as an idiosyncrasy in Indian culture. This is one of the reasons why there is almost no introspective literature in India and hardly any deep autobiographies that analyze motives and desires the way western autobiographies do. If idiosyncrasies are not worth thinking about, what do we think about if we want to think about ourselves? We can only think about what we share in common with our fellow human beings. That is, we think about the foundation. To reflect on one's Self is to reflect on the nature of human beings. If we are short tempered, greedy or whatever else, our reflections can only be about the nature of anger and the nature of greed. In short, as we go through life and to the extent we think about our Self, we are thinking about our fellow human beings and the psychology we all share. The further we push this reflection the more we understand human beings. So you see, the difference is that introspection focuses on the structure, self-knowledge focuses on the foundation. The experience that results from this thinking too is different: introspection generates pain and allied emotions; self-knowledge makes you wiser and happier. The first step, I believe, in learning to think about experience is to break free of the habit of introspection and stop reflecting on our individual thoughts, individual feelings and individual sensations.

Arya: But then how do I shake off this feeling that I am who I am because of my individual thoughts and feelings?

Leela: The cognitive strength of the Asian traditions lies in the fact that they do not merely tell us that such beliefs are illusory, but also show us why we live under this illusion and how we can break free. Right now, the dominant framework to understand the self is provided by the social sciences which do not do a good job of this at all. It is important to consider other frameworks without categorizing the ideas from the East as 'religious beliefs' and the ones from the West as 'social science'. The evidence, in fact, suggests quite the opposite.

Reeti: Actually, in my meditation experience I have often felt that there is no real self inside me, although I have only a fleeting experience of this state. It's as if the link between me and my actions does not really exist but that the actions are merely behavioral habit patterns that come into being because of a mental response to sensations. It's as if there is a super-imposition of an "I" on to an object or an action.

Leela: This link, of course, is the intentionality we've been talking about – the belief that we are agents with reasons and purposes. Through meditation we can learn not to conflate the structure of the 'I' with the structure of experience itself. Ignorance, then, is this conflation, while knowledge is becoming aware that the structure of our experience does not correspond to the structure of this narrative. When there is no continuous 'I' to be found in experience, it is obvious that there is no 'I' that is the agent of actions which are supposed to be the expressions of belief-states. There is just the organism and the actions. Of course, different Asian traditions give different accounts of this process.

Reeti: But then why do we always conflate the structure of the narrative about ourselves with the structure of our experience itself?

Leela: This attachment is necessary to have a stable experience of going about in the world. We can only examine a specific part of our experience and question the narrative that structures it. If we tried to undo this narrative for all parts of our experience at once, our experience would become total chaos. In fact, this is a problem that's applicable not just to the self but to any object or entity that persists over time. Because we speak of objects in terms of their existing in time and space, whether it involves disassembling and then reassembling a bicycle, or whether it is about a merger of two corporations, or whether it is about our own bodies, the logical problem of identity crops up. What makes any object the same object at different spatial and temporal intervals? We carry this problem over into discussions about psychological identity. For example, are you the same person you were when you were 5 years old? The theory of psychological identity tries to answer this question. To some extent, this is a valid problem and is carried over into the realm of law, ethics and society. For certain purposes, we need to assume that the issue of identity is not problematic. Otherwise we would not even be able to pay wages since you would not be the same person today as you were yesterday. Our social life will grind to a halt in the absence of some kind of convention about the social or psychological identity of a person. On the other hand, our self-representation or our image about ourselves which is believed to be our psychological identity gets in the way of truly knowing ourselves.

Arya: In that case, is it fair to say that psychoanalysis or behavioral therapy are the western counterparts to the *adhyatmic* aspects of the Indian traditions?

Leela: Of course! Speaking of psychoanalysis, what problem was Freud trying to solve? In its blandest form we can say that he was trying to solve whether one's experience about oneself and others, is true. If we keep in mind our discussion so far, it can be put even more provocatively: Is the experience of an individual directly accessible to the individual whose experience it is?

Arya: And of course he believed that it wasn't. He believed that you need a psychoanalyst to help you access your experience.

Leela: That's right; and he postulated many mechanisms to account for this non-accessibility. We need not get into the validity of his hypotheses, but the notion of experience and even the fact that we experience at all is of crucial importance to human beings. Such being the case, Freud's sensing of the 'problem-situation' is very sensitive indeed. The notion of experience has otherwise pretty much been ignored by western scholarship. Despite books and articles in many disciplines, the nature of experience is hardly studied. More often than not, it is reduced to thoughts, feelings, perception (or even sensation) and action. Thus, "what is experience?" remains an important question but very ill-understood. On the contrary, the Indian traditions made this 'problem-situation' a central focus of their enquiry. Naturally, they too discovered that experience is not 'true'; that there are things that prevent us from accessing these experiences. Different traditions called them by different names: *Maya, Avidya* or *Agyana*, are the best-known categories in this context. Removing this ignorance has been their central goal that would ultimately lead to *gyan udaya* or the 'arising of knowledge"; again, it is called by different names in different traditions. The hindrance to knowledge was seen as either a delusion of sorts or ignorance of sorts. One could eliminate this delusion, they said, and developed any number of practical ways of doing so. The plurality of the Indian traditions is partly a plurality of the ways of removing the veil of ignorance. In any case, these traditions too believed that some kind of mediation would be helpful in accessing one's experience. They called such a mediator a Guru and suggested that it would be helpful to have a Guru to achieve enlightenment.

Arya: In other words, it is the same problem situation with a radically different approach to resolving it.

Leela: Precisely. So you see, there exist two rival or competing practical traditions that provide different answers to the same problem situation. The Indian traditions challenge psychoanalytic and other psychological theories. Notice, however, that western scholars never looked at the issue in this manner. They insisted on bracketing the Indian traditions within a religious straitjacket. Why has the western world been blind to this very obvious connection and why do contemporary Indians merely repeat the western story that trying to access one's experience is a form of religion or spirituality?

This is one of the many ramifications of our colonial mindset. Right now in academia our only tools for delving into matters relating to man and society are those that are provided by the western social sciences. We need to question how useful these are in terms of understanding human psychology and human societies. What can we make of disciplines such as developmental psychology or clinical psychology which claim to study individual personalities scientifically when, in fact, they are basically working within a religious framework? It doesn't just stop there, of course. There is also the fact that the soul is closely related to the basic notion of 'agency' in law, ethics, micro-economics, and rational and social choice theories. So, you see, there is not just one problem but a bewildering variety of problems arising out of just this one concept. The implications of entertaining such a conception of the self are enormous.

Arya: I'm curious to see how this spills over into the other disciplines that you just mentioned. Can we explore some of these implications?

Leela: I can give you many random examples of different kinds to indicate the depth of the process in general. Consider the emergence of the legal system in western culture. The theologians of the Catholic Church turned to the Roman jurists in their attempts to build a legal structure for the church. This is called the famous 'Gregorian Reformation' of the Catholic Church. Thus arose a complex system of laws *and their justifications*, including terms that are fundamental to modern jurisprudence. This was called 'the canon law'. The civil law that we know of today was built by theologians by modeling it after the canon law. Till the 18th century, the faculty of law was a part of the faculty of theology in western universities and law was taught only by theologians. Consider, too, one of the notions fundamental to modern jurisprudence: the idea of 'will'. There have been umpteen discussions about this notion in philosophy, law and psychology. Clearly, or so the western world seems to think, human beings have a will and exercise it. But before the fourth century, this notion was absent in what we call western culture today. Neither the Greek thinkers, nor the Roman jurists had such a notion or such a picture of human beings. The first person to struggle with this notion and write tracts about it was Saint Augustine, one of the most influential fathers of the Christian church.

Reeti: Really? It's hard to imagine that this idea did not exist all along. What caused the shift, I mean, why did the Christians find the notion of will so important?

Leela: Because they believe that the universe exemplifies the will of God and that human beings should subordinate themselves to this will. What is human will then? What does this subordination consist of? These and many similar questions arose within the ambit of Christian theology, presupposing a Christian picture of man. A picture that was neither Greek nor Roman, and is most definitely not Indian. Yet how many of us do not practice law, read and write about the human will, and even assume *as an empirical fact* that it is in the nature of being human to have a will? This is no fact, but a Christian theological picture of man.

Reeti: But the idea of a will makes intuitive sense to most of us, including me, and I'm no Christian! It seems to be one of the most fundamental things about human beings. There must be some equivalent concept in the Indian traditions. We would not all be talking about exercising our free will if it wasn't even a thing.

Leela: There most definitely is no equivalent concept in the Indian traditions. Speaking of freedom, this concept is central to the western social sciences, in philosophy, in moral theories, in political theories, in legal theories, and psychological theories. To state it baldly in a single sentence: the idea is that it is a good thing that people are 'free' and that everyone ought to be free. In western ethical theories a moral action is an action of choice, made freely without coercion. In fact, according to western ethical theories, in the absence of 'freedom' morality is not possible. Now let's draw a contrast between this way of thinking and our ideas about karma and rebirth.

Arya: Good grief, I protest! Karma is baloney as far as I'm concerned and I don't see why I should give up one set of silly ideas only to take on another.

Leela: Calm down. You don't have to assume the truth of karma and rebirth to follow my point. I am not presenting these ideas as science. But you must acknowledge that they form a part of our folk psychology just as much as Biblical themes form a part of western folk psychology. I just want to use these concepts to draw a contrast between the idea of karma and the idea of free will. Karma, or the consequences of one's actions, supposedly tracks the agent across several lives. Somehow or the other, these notions are a part of our Indian understanding of morality. That means to say, if there was no binding and strict determinism, ethics would be impossible. Here, then, is the contrast: according to western culture, moral action is impossible if it is not 'free'; according to us, without strict determinism, moral action is impossible. So there are these two contrasting ways of looking at the same thing. Yet, all of us go about as though 'freedom' is a self-explanatory concept. It's actually not that evident. The origins of this theme can be found, you guessed it, in Christian theology. God created man and gave him the freedom to choose between God and the Devil. In more secularized terms it is called a choice between good and evil. The possibility of salvation, that is, of being saved from the clutches of the devil, depended on this free choice. Therefore, theological issues arose: what then does 'human freedom' mean? Why did God give freedom to man? Are we condemned to be free? And so on.

By contrast, our *svatantra* does not mean 'freedom' in this sense as its contrast term *paratantra* indicates. Our gods are '*sarva tantra svatantra*', that is, beings for whom all *tantras* (techniques) are *sva* (their own). This does not relate in any way to the structure of moral thinking in the West. Fundamental to Christianity is its belief that there ought to be scriptural sanction for actions. Unlike the Indian traditions, this religion makes one seek scriptural foundations for one's actions, whether for sacred ones like worshipping, or for secular ones like the attitude one should have regarding strangers. Scripture is one kind of revelation of God's will, Nature is another. People need to study both to find out what God wills so that they may become a part of God's purposes for human beings on earth.

Arya: Wait a second. What you're saying may have been true about a century ago. Today, very few people think in terms of scriptural sanctions. They act on principles that they believe in and not because God has anything to do with it.

Leela: Yes, but isn't this exactly what our whole discussion is about? The cognitive scheme set in place by God and religion is still intact even though we call it secular. Nothing's changed except for the vocabulary. Instead of God, folks now appeal to Reason or Principles *with the same attitude* as they had towards God. Remember, we already discussed that it is not at all clear that human action is based on reasons and principles. This is a pre-supposition based on Christian theology. In fact, the western system of ethics ties in snugly with its conceptualization of the self and rationality.

Reeti: How so?

Leela: The entire system of western ethics is built on the idea that all of us have a self and that it is rational for each individual to pursue their own individual interests. Since morality gets in the way of individual interests, we need to provide some justification before we can impose morals on society. This is what a theory of morals is supposed to provide. However, its recommendations do not depend upon the unique identity or circumstances of an individual but instead these recommendations are supposedly valid for all human beings at all times. That means to say, all the duties that a useful moral theory recommends are in the 'true interest' of each individual, all over the planet, irrespective of time or place or context.

Reeti: But how can you not have a context? There are all sorts of levels of importance. What about simple ethical rules like, say, "you should respond to your emails." Surely this type of rule is applicable in varying degrees and is therefore context-dependent.

Leela: It may appear to be so, but if you argue this out in the western scheme of things, as soon as you begin to question why one ought to respond to emails, the normative nature of this seemingly simple rule will become apparent. You will quickly see that the chain of arguments leads us to a universal norm from which this particular norm is derived.

Reeti: I don't think I get it. What do you mean by the normative nature of the rule?

Leela: The entire system of western ethics is built on norms. A norm is a moral rule with a characteristic structure that uses concepts like the moral 'ought' and the moral 'ought not'. For an action to be considered moral it must be susceptible to a description under a moral norm, based on which an action is considered to be either right or wrong. These norms hold irrespective of time, place, condition or the person. For instance, the norm that one ought not to torture is held to be true regardless of place, person, time, or culture. Even if torture is a practice common across all cultures, the validity of this statement is not affected. It tells us what 'ought not' to take place even if it does take place regularly. This is what is meant by normative thinking and the universal nature of norms. In western culture, the violation of a moral norm is considered immoral and following a moral norm is considered moral. This is the basic idea underlying the system of western ethics. Most Indians do not understand this type of ethics. At the same time, because these ideas sound and look very familiar we think we know what we are talking about. This too, is part of our colonial mindset.

Arya: But what is so wrong with a cognitive structure that results in beliefs that human beings ought not to torture? I'm sure there are similar norms in the Indian traditions, so what exactly is the difference?

Leela: It is important not to confuse the *ethical force* of some statements with norms. Indians do have many ways of expressing ethical statements but they are not normative because of that. There is only one way to recognize a normative ethical statement and that is by looking at its linguistic structure. Invariably, such statements make use of the word 'ought'. This 'ought' is the moral ought and we can recognize that it is a 'moral ought' because of its logical and linguistic properties. A distinction between 'what is the case' and 'what ought to be the case' distinguishes an empirical statement from a normative ethical statement. This mode of ethical reasoning does not exist in our culture. Such norms cannot even be formulated in the Indian languages! That is, we cannot say we 'ought not' to kill or we 'ought to' respect our parents, the way we can in the European languages. In our languages, such sentences have the same linguistic structure as an imperative like "you should not eat while walking", or as a conditional like "if you want to ace your test, you should study harder".

Arya: But how do you know that the 'should' in our languages does not have the same logical and semantic properties that the moral 'ought' has in the European languages?

Leela: It's simple. There are systems of Deontic Logics (anyone with some understanding of the mathematical model theory can follow them) that very precisely delineate the property and behavior of moral concepts like 'forbidden', 'obligatory', or 'permissible'. By linguistic analysis we can show that the Indian equivalents do not exhibit this logical and semantic behavior. The system of ethics in Indian culture works without norms. In none of the Indian languages is it possible to distinguish either logically or linguistically between the statements "you must not do something" and you "ought not to do something". If we had normative ethics, then our languages would contain a word that does what the moral 'ought' does in western culture.

In fact, there is some very interesting research by Henry Rosemont that shows that in the classical Chinese language there are no words corresponding to 'moral', 'individual', 'utility', 'rationality', 'objective', 'subjective, 'choice', 'dilemma', 'duty', 'rights', or even 'ought'. That means that in classical Chinese it is not possible to speak of 'moral duty' or 'moral dilemmas' or 'moral choices'. It is not even possible to formulate a rule which uses the notions of 'ought' – either obligatory ("all ought to do x") or prudential ("if one desires x, then one ought to do y"). By contrast, in the western intellectual tradition, the 'essence' of a moral principle or norm is that it is formulated using the 'ought', either in the obligatory or prudential form. Without 'ought', there would be no difference in kind between factual and evaluative statements. Yet it is impossible to do precisely that in Confucianism. And Confucians, by all accounts, were clearly concerned about human conduct and the good life.

Reeti: But our *dharma shastras* speak about *dharma* as being constituted by injunctions and prohibitions. So, for example, they say that such and such ritual 'must' be performed. Or such and such action 'should not' be done. Isn't there a moral ought implicit in this statement? How else can we understand it?

Leela: Understand it as a simple instruction for action. Or, to look at it another way, in the eastern traditions there is no link between morality and the truth of any proposition or principle. By contrast, in the West morality is primarily derived from, or is seen as the expression of, holding correct moral principles. Moreover, these principles are held to be true at all times for all people. They specify what ought to be the case, even if it is not the case.

Reeti: But why can't the 'ought' in the western system of ethics be regarded in the same way as we Indians regard 'should' or 'must'?

Leela: This is because it is typical of normative statements that one *ought not to* violate them under any circumstances, even if one does so regularly. If you think that they can be violated depending upon the circumstances, then this would be tantamount to claiming that there is no ethical domain to talk about.

Reeti: I'm still having a problem understanding this. In any case, we ought not to torture, whether this is a normative belief or a non-normative one. Is it problematic because of the fact that people do torture in any case so ethical theories lose their credibility and begin to sound more like rationalizations?

Leela: Normative claims can never be derived from purely factual premises because the step from fact to norm is a leap which cannot be sustained by factual reasoning. When we discuss ethical norms, we do not rely on factual premises but different kind of premises which are themselves normative. In other words, you cannot go from what *is the case* to what *ought to be the case* in any objective way.

The only way to understand how western culture came to be swept up by normative ethics is to look at the religion that shaped this culture. The emergence of the ethical domain in the course of western history is linked to God's will for humanity. We saw how God's will fuses causes and reasons. Whatever God wills is not only good but it also comes into being. Therefore, whatever exists is also how it ought to be. This is how God's will unites the factual and the normative. In the real world the factual and the normative can never be united. But because of this theological idea lurking in the background, it seems *plausible* in western culture to suggest that human behavior can be based on norms. This also explains why India (or Asia, generally) does not have normative categories or why we do not have normative ethics. Naturally, many ethical norms such as "All human beings ought to be free and equal" carry a force that

we learn to identify with. We learn to rally strong emotions when such claims are made. We feel as though all
problems of injustice in the world would disappear if
only all human beings were 'free' and 'equal'. However,
in reality, these moral emotions prevent us from thinking critically about such accounts. The normative world
is a separate world that is immune to all factual considerations. I believe it would benefit our debates on such
issues if we were to dispose of normative thinking. Besides, the presence of norms in a human community
does not tell us anything about whether these norms do,
in fact, govern the behavior of the members of the community.

Reeti: I don't know about you, but I feel like it is a good thing
to have certain universal norms that prevent cruelty and
injustice and that everyone should strive to live by.

Leela: But the universalizability of norms does not mean that
people actually factually follow these norms. Even if
everyone tells lies, the ethical statement "one ought not
to lie" is a universal moral statement. The very existence
of debates about, say, abortion or war is indicative of the
nature of normative rules. Because 'one ought not to
kill', debates and doctrines about 'justified war' come
into being. It is important to note that these doctrines do
not contradict the injunction not to kill but instead provide justifications for undertaking such an 'immoral' action. They provide the mitigating circumstances, so to
speak.

Arya: The other problem I can see under this scenario is that if
morality is a question of applying the right principles
and if there are conflicting principles what would happen to the status of the norms?

Leela: Under some theory or the other you can always do anything. This situation has been blessed and sanctified
with the label of 'pluralism'. When people have different moral judgments about the same problem like, say,

the death penalty, they all feel equally certain about their judgments. So how do we solve such moral disagreements? If the notion of morality is such that all you can have is either an 'ethically good' or an 'ethically bad' or an 'ethically neutral' action, the demand is always to provide one of these. If such neatly packaged actions are not available, what are the consequences? You do exactly what you feel like with the realization that you could always defend the action as an ethically good one. Even genocides can, and have been, based on sound ethical reasoning.

Arya: I suppose this is why moral talk so often comes across as pure rhetoric. In fact it sounds like a license to act immorally while feeling sanctimonious at the same time. This also accounts for the grotesque fact that in the West, some very smart people end up having some very stupid discussions like "would you kill one fat man to save three skinny ones" in all seriousness! But how did the entire western world fall into the clutches of normative thinking?

Leela: The roots of this can be traced back to the Protestant Reformation. Before the Reformation, the Catholic Church and its priests acted as mediators between God and the believers. The Protestants broke with the Catholic religion by insisting that no mediation was required between God and the believers and that the duties of the priests and monks were the duties of all Christians. The long, drawn out, and intense process of arguing that the Bible commands all believers, in the same way, for all time, led to the gradual emergence and spread of normative ethics in the form we are familiar with today. Although there have been revivals of pagan notions of ethics such as 'virtue' ethics, and supererogatory ethics (that which goes over and beyond the call of duty), the basic mode of thinking about ethics in the western world remains normative. Even though the problems it tries to solve are 'secular', the cognitive structure of normative ethics is directly inherited from problems in Christian theology.

Reeti: What alternative ways are there to work out ethical quandaries? What is the structure of the moral domain if it is not defined by norms? For instance, how are ethical judgments arrived at among Indians if there are no norms?

Leela: Unlike western ethical theories that differentiate between the moral domain and the non-moral one, in India there is no specific moral domain and no specific moral norms. Every action that you perform is an action within the 'moral' domain. For instance, the notion of *dharma* is all-encompassing and, in fact, is not just limited to human beings.

Reeti: This does not make any sense. The fact that we're just sitting here sipping our *chai* is not something that can be considered to be a part of the moral domain.

Leela: The most fundamental category of 'moral judgment' in the Indian traditions is that of appropriateness. That is, some action is 'moral' or 'immoral' depending upon whether or not it is appropriate or inappropriate. The Indian notion of ethics also ties in with its notion of the 'self'. Let's say you are a biological organism interacting within the framework of a community. This community consists of various institutions that divide up your life into easily recognizable gestalts or forms: that is, you may be a friend, a daughter, a father, a teacher, a doctor, or a pupil. To be a son within this community means to give *form* to many actions typical of this gestalt. A human being is made up of several of these gestalts. They function as a sort of a minimum common denominator that suggests that by virtue of performing certain types of actions some organism is recognized to be a mother or a daughter or a friend. It is important to emphasize that these gestalts are not pictures of an ideal daughter or an ideal mother. Nor do they fully specify what it means to be a daughter or a mother. Notice, however, that unlike in the western world, there is no *reason* for which a person ought to perform any particular daughter-type or mother-type action. The behavior is not rationalized based on some principle. Rather, what we consider as ethics (the non-normative variety) takes human well-being as the goal and defines ethical thinking as the process of reflection on what this is and how to achieve it.

Arya: So we don't follow rules or norms, but just live up to certain ideas of what it means to behave in a certain way that promotes well-being? But if there are no rules or norms, then how are ethical disputes settled?

Leela: The community provides the standards. The relation is not between an individual and some moral rule but rather the relation is between individuals and the communities they are a part of. The idea of a moral individual presupposes a moral community. As we already discussed, the medium of education and socialization in India is predominantly that of stories. To belong to a community is to share this basic repertoire of stories. There are many, many, types of stories and given that we find ourselves in different situations, there would be as many moral ideals as our different 'stations' in life. By the same token, what would be seen as a moral ideal for a homemaker cannot be seen as one for a student; or a moral ideal for a *sadhu* cannot be seen as one for a businessman. In this sense, to speak of a moral ideal that is applicable to everybody, the way one does in the West, is literally senseless when viewed from within the context of Indian culture.

Arya: If the justification for moral actions is based on a repertoire of stories that model such actions, sooner or later this will generate some norms that will be the same as the kind of moral norms that the West is familiar with.

Leela: But the stories do not set any absolute standard that embodies some value using which some action could be branded moral or immoral. Rather, stories sketch out different ways of acting so that judgments about appropriateness are always relative to being able to propose an alternative action.

Reeti: I think I understand. Remember the story about the monkey and the flood? I just thought of it because I recall that some of my American friends found it disturbing and even distasteful, but most Indians do not have a problem with such stories. I think this may be because we are more conditioned to being responsive to context rather than looking at principles or morals outside of a context.

Arya: I don't think I know this story.

Reeti: It's the one about the monkey with a small baby who got swept off in a terrible flood. As the flood waters kept on rising she tried desperately to find a safe haven for herself and her little baby. She struggled up a hill, but the waters came swirling furiously up. In a frenzy she scrambled on top of the highest rock on the hill, only to see the waters keep on reaching up. She then placed her baby on her shoulders, watching in horror as the waters kept on rising till they rose all the way up to her shoulders. Frantic, she stood up on her tiptoes, but alas, the waters reached right up to her nostrils. In a final act of despair, she took her baby off her shoulders, placed it on the rock beneath her feet, and stood upon it. And that's the story!

Leela: This should make it clear why it does not make sense to spell out morals based on stories. Stories do their work in other ways. Actions are not depicted as being either moral or immoral as such, even though they are susceptible to being ordered as 'less moral', 'less immoral' or whatever. In such a conceptualization, moral and immoral cease to be classificatory concepts as is the case in western moral theories.

Reeti: Now I'm on a roll! I think I recognize this pattern in many other stories. I recently watched an episode from the *Shiva Purana* that was about the upcoming wedding of Shiva and Parvati. Before the wedding, Parvati goes to Shiva and pleads with him that he must dress properly and look nice for the wedding ceremony. Shiva responds by saying that he likes living the way he does, and that suiting up in formal attire would make him feel very stuffy. They carry on back and forth along these lines, with Parvati pleading that her family would be horrified to see his matted locks and ash-smeared body, and Shiva insisting that he must remain true to his nature. Of course, there are equally cogent arguments from both sides and you're left wondering if the matter is ever going to get resolved. Luckily this one has a happy ending as far as I'm concerned, because in the end Shiva does end up getting all spruced up and wearing nice clothes for the wedding.

Leela: It's important to note that the same arguments can also be cast in normative terms relating to what each person 'ought to' be doing. In fact, when we speak in English about ethics, we are invariably forced into normative language with strict categories of right and wrong. Western intellectuals reason about ethics exclusively in normative terms. Notice, however, that our intuitions tell us that both Shiva and Parvati are right in a moral sense. Making sense of such possibilities is what non-normative ethics is all about.

Reeti: So non-normative ethics is not based on reasons, even if it does use reasoning to support its arguments. I guess, this is also how we can understand Krishna's advice in the *Mahabharata*, for instance, when he tells the Pandavas to break the rules of warfare and attack after sunset and to strike Duryodhana below the belt. When viewed from a normative perspective it sounds immoral to break the rules, but nobody really feels that way when we actually hear the story. It cannot be that we all support immoral behavior, so it must have something to do with the framework we use in looking at such things.

Leela: That's right. In the Indian framework, the stories depict the fallibility of moral rules by setting up moral choices between moral principles themselves. Following some moral rule is possible only by violating some other moral rule. On this picture, the very notion of a moral rule must incorporate its fallible character so that no moral rule is either obligatory or forbidden under all circumstances. By contrast, in the western normative framework, being obligatory or being forbidden are considered crucial properties of all moral statements. It is also important to note that under the western framework of normative ethics, the moral ideal is unreachable because the suggestion is that everyone is imperfect. This is not the case in the Indian context because the fallibility lies in the moral rules and not in the person.

Reeti: Speaking of the obligatory nature of western ethics, I kind of sense this whenever I hear people from the West talk about the Asian traditions. Everything they say seems to take on a normative moral quality. The confusion of the self with the body is no longer seen as a cognitive mistake that leads to unhappiness but rather as something that falls exclusively in the moral domain. It's made to sound like having an 'ego' is a sin of some kind rather than an expression of ignorance about the self.

Leela: That's true. The most basic point to consider is this: What are morals and ethics useful for? Are we supposed to learn to categorize which type of action is ethical or are we supposed to learn how to act ethically? Normative ethics does not address how to generate courses of action but rather points out what is moral and what is not. It sees an ethical event as one that requires a decision procedure, or making choices as it is popularly referred to. So even if you figure out what the right action is, you still have the problem of performing the right action.

In the Indian traditions an ethical event requires an action heuristic or rule of thumb. Philosophers carry on and on about the universalizability of moral rules, the 'is-ought' problem, or the nature of the 'good' without even pausing to reflect whether the very idea of the ethical domain itself varies across cultures. And we Indians, of course, act like the only road to salvation is through ideas derived from the western social sciences. I hope it's becoming clear how we have systematically and steadily shut out all alternatives for ourselves. Almost every English-educated Indian claims to understand western normative ethics. This has become our only language of ethics to the extent that an alternative conceptualization of the ethical domain seems almost inconceivable. But this normative conception of ethics is inadequate to describe our ethical experience. In fact it can only suppress this experience. We are so profoundly bewitched by western culture and so thoroughly insulated from our own that we've become ignorant of our own ignorance. And this is not all, of course. There are many, many other ways in which we limit ourselves by blindly aping the West.

Reeti: How depressing! On the positive side, becoming aware of our problems is a huge step in itself. It sounds like we may have many more items on the agenda. May I suggest that we take a break for now and save our discussions for later?

CHAPTER VI

HOW SECULAR IS SECULARISM?

Arya: Last evening's conversation has got to have been one of the most fascinating ones I've ever had in my life. My head was buzzing so much with these ideas that I could barely bring myself to sleep. But it also left me wondering about some things. I think that in every culture the foundations of knowledge must have been laid by a specific segment in society. Do you think the Brahmins in India played a role similar to that of the theologians in the West? Are we too, in our own way, in the grips of some sort of junk science?

Leela: The Brahmins do not play a role in Indian society that even remotely resembles that of the priests, rabbis or mullahs. Nor did they ever have any kind of overarching influence in society to disseminate a specific type of knowledge throughout the land. This is a development unique to western culture. The Catholic Church confronted many social and political problems during its history. Whether it was a revolt of the peasants or a fight with the monarchs about the nature of political authority, these phenomena were conceptualized as problems *within theology*. These very same questions and answers, and the underlying framework, have been taken over by the social sciences. When they continue along this track, all they do is embroider Christian theology further. No matter what they think they are doing, they are not doing science. Western intellectuals are blind to secularized theology, because that is all they know. This is their tool to understand man and society, and there is no other. What's worse is that we too have adopted these tools for understanding our culture and our society.

Only when we develop alternate ways of theorizing about man and society will we be able to grasp the theological nature of this way of thinking. When that happens, it will truly be a revolution in human thinking. Then we can begin to speak in terms of the *sciences* of the social. Until such time, all we have are obscure theologies masquerading as the social sciences.

Arya: I agree whole-heartedly that it's important to develop alternatives to the current social sciences. In the meantime we can focus on the positive things that we have gotten from them. At least we can be grateful for such things as democracy and secularism.

Leela: I wouldn't be so sure about that. It's a well-known fact that for many centuries there were relatively stable and peaceful societies throughout Asia with a diversity of traditions far greater than Europe has ever known. In light of this, on what grounds can we claim that the solution to India's problems can be found only in the principles of western liberal theories? In fact, a number of studies have shown that secularism has not helped in quelling religious strife in India. If anything, it has made matters worse and we must figure out why this is the case. To compound our problems, the word 'secularism' has turned into a mantra that we keep repeating without being able to make much sense of it. This is not particularly surprising because the very idea of secularism is rooted in a theology that most Indians have no knowledge of.

Arya: It matters not a whit that this idea has its origins in foreign theologies that we don't know much about. The idea stands on its own merits.

Leela: I don't mean to suggest that you have to read the Bible before you can understand anything that comes out of the West. My point is that in the West one knows what 'religion' and the 'secular state' refer to because these terms are embedded in a common background framework. This background framework reflects a shared cultural and historical experience that puts limits on the interpretation of words by relating concepts to each other in systematic ways. When these concepts and principles migrate from one cultural setting to another, they get detached from this background framework and begin to lose their basic intelligibility. This is what happens in the Indian secularism debates. There is no shared background framework that places limits on the interpretation of terms and principles. Consequently, even where we adopt the exact blueprints of western political thought, these are interpreted in random ways. This leads to semantic distortion and obscurity. In short, most Indians have no idea what they're talking about when they talk about secularism.

Reeti: But we all agree that the word 'secularism' means something different in India. In fact, as we've been discussing all along, people look at things through the framework they are familiar with. Indians have their own framework so naturally many words have different meanings for us. I don't see why we cannot look at secularism from a historical context as it pertains specifically to India. After all, there is no single true model of a secular state even in the West.

Leela: This type of argument abounds with confusion. For example, let's say we were talking about 'ice cream' and let's say you believe that ice cream means different things to different people. It means a 'treat' to one and 'fattening' to another and so on. You could even say that it means different things to the same individual at different points in their life. So far, so good. But the problem is this: These different meanings of 'ice cream' presuppose that we're talking about the same thing. Only under this condition can we say that 'ice cream' means different things to different people. To make sure we're talking about the same thing, we need a reference for the word. In many cases, such as with words like 'secularism', it is a linguistic description of the word that provides us with the reference. But under no circumstances can it be a different description for different people.

The concept of secularism comprises a specific way of organizing relations between political organizations and religious institutions. When we say that France, Belgium, and India are all secular states, we're basically saying that we attribute certain *common* properties to these states even if these countries have developed different forms of the secular state. Our problems have nothing to do with the fact that secularism means one thing on the European continent, something else in Africa, and something altogether different in India. The truth is that our use of this word is merely a learned way of talking that we've picked up from our colonial masters without much reflection. In the minds of many Indians, secularism indeed means something different. What it means, however, is totally unclear.

Reeti: I think that when we talk about secularism, we basically mean to say that it involves seeing all religions as equal.

Leela: But we cannot just concoct any meaning we feel like without taking into consideration how concepts relate to each other! The idea that all religions are equal cannot possibly be accepted by Muslim and Christian believers. The very foundation of Islam and Christianity suggests that these religions are the unique revelation of God. Therefore, they have to distinguish between themselves as the true religion and others as false religion. Moreover, the idea that all religions are equal is a barren description of the Indian attitude towards the variety of human traditions. It can never serve as a hypothesis which could refine our understanding of traditional Indian pluralism. The current stories about religion and secularism in India endlessly keep adding *ad hoc* modifications to the dominant account of religion. This has resulted in a conceptual muddle that does not allow us to locate the problems or to even make sense of our experience. As a consequence we are unable to challenge the dominant theoretical framework.

Arya: That may be. But you cannot deny that the idea of secularism is a profoundly ethical one, and therefore worth pursuing.

Leela: On the surface, the project of secularism indeed seems to be profoundly ethical. But in reality there is no evidence that secularism has strengthened the fabric of Indian society. To the extent that it may have made matters worse, it would be unethical *not to question* this principle. Once we begin to challenge the cognitive grounds for the belief in secularism and to question why these are held to be more ethical than what our indigenous cultural traditions have to offer, we will not be able to come up with any answers. In fact, the concept of secularism poses many problems even in the religious cultures that it originated in. When transferred on to the Indian context, these problems are further exacerbated resulting in one unholy mess.

Reeti: What cognitive problems does this concept entail exactly?

Leela: First of all, it is a normative model rather than a pragmatic or prudential one. Because it is normative, it relates to facts in a peculiar way. We've already touched upon this, but the basic conceptual flaw in the western liberal notion of secularism is its division of the world into two spheres. The secular model claims that the state should be neutral in terms of religion and that the state's policies and legal system cannot be based on any religious doctrine. On the other hand, this model insists that the right to religious freedom should be granted to all citizens. Each citizen ought to be free to worship as they please, and everyone should respect this freedom and tolerate each other's forms of religious belief or unbelief. In this way, the model divides plural societies into two spheres: a political or public sphere, where citizens are subject to the laws of the state, and a religious or private sphere, where they ought to be free to live according to their values or conceptions of the good life.

Arya: Sounds good to me. I don't see the problem.

Leela: The problem lies in its lack of conceptual clarity. Although secularism showed promise in the West by effectively resolving the constant religious strife among those who shared a religious framework, it has not produced the same results in non-western cultures. For starters, there is no clarity on what counts as religion and how to go about distinguishing the religious from the secular. The dominant 'religion' of India is supposed to be Hinduism, but there is no clarity as to what Hinduism is, whether it is a religion or not, or whether it even exists. If you cannot even identify it, how can you separate it from the state? There is no organization that serves as an authority that can speak on behalf of this entity called Hinduism. Consequently, the burden falls on the courts to determine whether some practice is a religious practice or not. In this way we end up bestowing upon our secular judges a religious authority far greater than that of any high priest!

Arya: This does sound odd, I must admit. Not only because religious matters are not exactly the area of expertise of secular judges, but it also violates one of the fundamental tenets of secularism – the principle of separation which requires that the authority of each ought to remain confined to their own realm.

Leela: You see, there are no *secular* criteria that enable one to identify the sphere of religion in a manner that is neutral to all religions. What ends up happening is that a specific religious language, that is, the language of Protestant Christianity, becomes the standard language to discuss matters of religion in courts of law. This calls into question the very claim to religious neutrality at the heart of the liberal model.

Arya: Actually, now that you mention it, I can see that secularism throws up similar problems in the western world too. We cannot just assume that human lives have a natural dual structure even if in the western world the division is more clear-cut.

Leela: This appears to be a basic flaw in the secular model. It does indeed pose several problems when you detach the idea from its explicitly religious roots.

Reeti: Can you give us the background of the specific religious roots in this case?

Leela: Indeed, a bit of background will help to understand what the problem is really about. Ever since the earliest history of Christianity, it was believed that the world is split into two different realms: the spiritual and the temporal. The spiritual world was equated with the clergy and God, and the temporal world comprised of regular human beings referred to as the laity (or laymen). Christian doctrine claims that each individual has a soul and that this soul should endeavor to become as spiritual as possible. It was the duty of human beings to turn away from the carnal or temporal world in which we human beings live and turn towards the spiritual world of God. From Augustine to Aquinas, the dominant political thought in Europe took this two-fold division of human existence as its starting point. Then came the Protestant Reformation of the sixteenth century that transformed the religious landscape dramatically. Whereas, up until now, the spiritual and the temporal had been equated with the clergy and the laity respectively, Reformation theology claimed that there could be no such hierarchical division among believers. The spiritual estate could not be considered to be the exclusive domain of the priests, as opposed to a temporal estate comprising of laymen. Since all human beings were equal in the

eyes of God, each individual had the freedom to interpret God's will for themselves and no human being, including the Pope, the priests, or the magistrates, could
extend their authority into the spiritual sphere of religion. God alone could be the judge. Notice, however,
that even though this Protestant theology removed the
distinction that had made the spiritual domain the exclusive domain of the priests, it still retained the two-fold
division of a spiritual realm and a temporal realm.

Reeti: Okay, but this sounds mostly like a spiritual doctrine.
How does it relate to the political doctrine?

Leela: As I just said, according to Protestants, the religious
sphere which pertains to the domain of the soul can be
ruled and judged by God alone and thus must be free
from all human laws. This *freedom from human laws* is
what the Protestants called 'Christian liberty'. Each individual had the liberty of conscience to make their own
laws in the religious realm, as this, they believed, was
God's will for humanity. It is this theological scheme
that was then carried over into the political and social
realm and has basically structured our thinking about the
world for the past five centuries.

Arya: I see. In modern terminology, this amounts to the claim
that there has to be a separation of church and state.

Leela: Precisely. We no longer talk about the sinful body that
should be disciplined by law, or the spiritual soul that
should be free to turn to God; we no longer talk about
the division of the world into temporal and spiritual
realms. But these ideas continue to lurk in the background and without their presence it is impossible to
make sense of the contemporary notion of secularism.
Today's liberal society still accepts this division of the
spheres, although the somewhat controversial value of
individual autonomy is now replaced by the idea of neutrality. And instead of religious and temporal, we talk in
secularized terminology about private and public

spheres. But that's all that it is – a change in vocabulary, nothing more. The conceptual structure is still that of Protestant Christianity although it is presented as if it is something neutral.

Reeti: It's now becoming clearer and clearer what you meant when you said that the secular world is still a religious world. Among the believers the religious claims are straightforward and in the foreground; among the non-believers these same religious ideas lurk in the background and lend intelligibility to 'secular' ideas. But again, couldn't we say that this is nevertheless a practical solution and in general it is not a bad idea to separate things into the private sphere and the public sphere?

Leela: If we look beyond the superficialities, we will most likely not be able to find a coherent way to form this division into spheres. For instance, most people will say that their bedroom belongs in the private sphere and that the state and its legal machinery ought not to interfere there. But then they will quickly change their mind if they discover that a particular bedroom is the scene of domestic abuse or child abuse and so the state and its legal machinery ought to interfere. Has this particular bedroom suddenly moved from the private to the public sphere? There are innumerable similar examples to show that people are not able to distinguish between the political/public and the religious/private. There is no satisfactory way to tell what characterizes the religious realm as opposed to other realms in society. Do things such as inheritance law, diet, and mode of dress belong in the private religious sphere or in the public sphere? How can we be neutral in judging, for instance, whether a man's beard belongs in the religious realm or if it is merely the manifestation of some hipster fad? The contemporary social sciences cannot provide us with a satisfactory standard to make any such distinction. When the courts are required to rule on such things, the difference becomes subjective. Of course people talk as if the concept is crystal clear and this influences how we experience our lives as being divided into a public life and a private life. The model of the secular liberal state compels us to invoke this distinction. It also shapes the legal and political structures in many parts of the world. However, this does not imply that the division is real. Throughout human history, all kinds of policies and models of society have been built on wrong ideas and fictitious entities. Things do not become real just because a majority of the people think they are real.

Reeti: It does seem to be much more problematic than one would have thought. One cannot endorse the idea of secularism without also endorsing the Biblical view that the world is divided into two separate realms. In the Indian context, this makes very little sense. It would be akin to endorsing the claim that we need to separate *dharma* from politics!

Leela: The problem goes much deeper than that. When we adopt a secular doctrine we are compelled to describe our indigenous Indian traditions in a manner that accords with the truth claims of the Abrahamic religions. Our traditions *have to be absorbed* into the framework set by Judaism, Christianity and Islam.

Arya: I agree with all of this. But our goal is to work towards a peaceful, diverse, and viable society free from communal violence. Secularism allows us to work towards such goals and provides us with a framework to deal with communal violence. As a believer in secularism, I strongly feel we ought to separate politics from religion as best we can because, without such a separation, the state cannot treat all religions in at least somewhat of a neutral manner.

Leela: But if an idea is not conceptually sound then any policies it spawns will reflect its shortcomings. It can never be neutral because it is based on Protestant theology, so it is pointless talking about secularism as something that is enshrined in diversity. Since you mention communal violence, let's look at one of the hot button issues relating to communal violence – the problem of religious conversion. Hopefully, this will demonstrate the conceptual muddle that results from a collision between divergent understandings of religion, tradition, secularism, and freedom of religion.

Reeti: I would love to have some clarity on this matter. I think it's safe to say that most Hindus have an attitude of outright aversion to conversion. The very idea seems wrong somehow. What bothers me about the conversion debates in India is that this feeling is characterized as some sort of hardcore Hindu fundamentalism. But it cannot be that Hindus are fundamentalists just because they don't relate to the concept of conversion. What makes it even more confusing is that in India the secular liberals sound exactly like the evangelical fundamentalists of the United States when it comes to matters relating to conversion. Speaking for myself, I feel like my aversion to conversion taps into something distinctly 'Indian', but I cannot articulate this feeling properly. I would like to have a better understanding of the conceptual issues involved in conversion instead of just treating this as a political matter.

Leela: There are no real conceptual problems when we talk about the conversion of Christians to Islam or the other way round. The conceptual problems arise when it involves the conversion of Hindus into Christianity or Islam. This entails a confrontation between two very different ways of going about in the world. The call for conversion imposes a model of 'religion as belief' which is alien to the indigenous traditions of India.

Reeti: It's no wonder that the Christian missionaries have always found it frustrating that Hindus merely shrug their shoulders and say that Christian beliefs may be good for Christians but this does not mean that they are applicable for everybody. Hindus have never confronted Christians as rivals on this account or tried to convince them that their beliefs are all wrong.

Leela: In reality, the proselytizing drive in Christianity and Islam, and the Hindu attitude that 'all religions are true', indicates a deep conflict of values. A Christian or Muslim believer sees it as their moral duty to save people from eternal damnation by ensuring that they don't worship false gods. To them, 'freedom of religion' means the freedom to preach and make converts to their 'true' religion. To the Hindu, all gods and all religions are 'true' and they regard attempts at conversion as a form of interference with their traditions. Both sides end up feeling violated because there is no neutral ground between the two premises that no religion is false and that some religions are false.

Arya: But the fact that Hindus are now busy trying to re-convert Muslims and Christians back into the Hindu fold indicates how deeply entrenched they have become in the framework of Islam and Christianity. Otherwise, from the traditional Indian perspective, the idea that a false religion should be replaced by a true religion does not make any sense.

Leela: That is true, but the contemporary reality is that we do face problems on account of conversion and the state has to deal with them somehow. Because there is no neutral position with respect to conversion, the state has to come out on one side of the issue or the other. As we know, the Indian state has decided to address this problem through the framework of the religious-secular distinction presented by the Abrahamic religions, which makes no sense in the context of the Indian traditions.

Reeti: What a mess! This means that even though the state does not accept the specific truth claims of any religion, it does assume that religion revolves around beliefs and truth claims. In this way the Indian state reproduces

Christian themes even while it claims to be taking a neutral position. There's got to be a better way that takes into account the various heathen traditions, that exist as the majority in India, and that do not share the anthropology of the Abrahamic religions. It could just be that we have a different way of looking at the truth. It is not so much about being true or false as it is about a pluralistic approach.

Leela: It's true that the English-speaking Indians have learned to talk in terms of religion and truth in their own peculiar way but this does not mean that it holds up to logic. Historically, the pagan traditions have tried to make sense of the Abrahamic claims about religious truth from their own traditional perspectives. The result is the oft-repeated claim that 'all religions are true'. I think that this just indicates an attempt to translate the attitude of one culture into the language of another, nothing more than that.

Arya: But I feel like there can be no going back now. Secularism is a good idea in situations where we want to curb any form of tyranny from the dominant religion of the region. I'm apprehensive about the rise of Hindu fundamentalism, with its threat to intellectual freedom. A secular stance can keep it under control.

Reeti: I'm amazed how you're always ready to jump on Hindu fundamentalism when it's quite clear that the secular stance has never even tried to take the indigenous Indian experience into account. Nor have Indian secularists contributed to any progress towards communal harmony.

Leela: As I've repeatedly been saying, in India, both secularism and Hindu fundamentalism are two sides of the same coin. They are both a result of colonialism and our colonial consciousness. You see, our colonial masters came up with several descriptions of Indian cultural practices, all of which started with the assumption that

Indian culture was inferior to that of the West. Secularism was set in contrast to this picture as a moral and rational replacement for the immoral and irrational Indian culture. This colonial legacy is carried forward by our current crop of Indian secularists who pretty much share the colonial attitude that the ills of India are essentially related to Hinduism. These people have dominated the Indian universities and established an institutional hegemony that performs a role very similar to that of our colonial masters. The growth of fundamentalism is a direct result of this coercive straitjacket. As Hindus began to feel like they were being robbed of their voices, they went on the defensive. Unfortunately, when they began to articulate a defense of their traditions, this did not take the form of reflections on Hindu tradition or its ability to address the problems of modern society. Instead, it took the form of a militant defense of their traditions. As a result, the traditional Hindu tolerance is giving way to an increasingly shrill and aggressive voice. The self-confidence and vibrancy of our traditions has turned into a fanatical defense of its 'religious' doctrines.

Arya: Be that as it may, I think it's safe to say that at this point all religions look at each other as rivals, whether Hindu, Muslim or Christian. The historical and conceptual background is interesting but I'm not sure how relevant it is in our contemporary context.

Leela: We better believe it is relevant if we don't want a bad situation to get worse. When pursued systematically, state policies are bound to have an impact on society. As far as I can tell, it has not been a good one. Therefore, it is very relevant to question our state policies in this context. By assuming the truth of Abrahamic theological claims, the Indian state actively creates and sustains opposition between religions and traditions. It transforms a conflict between different groups into a religious conflict and coerces communities to resolve their internal conflicts in a religious manner. By taking this stance, the secular state in India does not prevent religious fanaticism, it actively promotes it.

Reeti: Speaking of fanaticism, I think there's something fundamentally wrong with the way all fanatical movements are seen as variants of the same phenomenon. Whether we're talking about Islamic fanaticism in the Arab world, Christian fundamentalism in the United States, the *Hindutva* movement in India, violent Buddhist groups in Sri Lanka or Burma, or the assorted militant movements in Africa, all of the analyses presuppose that they can all be classified into two broad categories: liberal secular movements on one hand and religious fundamentalists on the other. There's got to be something wrong with this total absence of nuance.

Leela: We certainly lack any fruitful understanding of these various movements. It's not as though the modern liberal compares two cultural cognitive schemes in a scientific manner and then concludes that one is better and should replace the other. No, they simply assume the moral and cognitive superiority of their own social and political theories. This provides them with a framework that justifies the destruction of cultural practices on the basis of a deeply flawed understanding of them. It wipes out cultural practices without even examining their cognitive or cultural value to humanity and replaces them with western legal structures whose value to humanity we have never even begun to question.

Reeti: That's so true. I find it interesting that before the British enforced a legal framework in India, social life was never governed by codified laws. There were no laws outlawing drugs, homosexuality, prostitution, abortion, or suicide, for example. Nevertheless, all hell did not break loose because of an absence of laws. In fact, our culture and society could only have been described as deeply conservative. Things like marriage were elaborate social customs that did not require any legal endorsement on a piece of paper. The introduction of a legal structure to govern social practices seems to have had more of a corrupting influence than a beneficial one. It would be so much more worthwhile to figure out how to strengthen the fabric of society rather than to keep introducing one law after another.

Leela: It would indeed be very worthwhile to study our traditional ways of coping with the problems of society and for living in harmony. India does not need secularism for its survival. Hindus, Muslims, Christians, Jews, and several other groups were quite successful in living together in relative peace for long periods of time in India. This plural society did not fall apart. Yet, it had never even heard of 'secularism' or 'toleration,' let alone implemented secular liberal democracy.

Reeti: Do we know if there was any systemized form of knowledge in India that examined ways of living together? I thought that the British made laws in India based on our own cultural and social practices.

Leela: Much of our indigenous forms of knowledge were enshrined in treatises like the *Dharma Shastra*. These contain a variety of reflections, sayings, and maxims for settling disputes based on the customs of different groups of people. But they were never considered to be binding rules of law. Instead of allowing these to play the role in society as they had always done, the British began to codify them into a systematic, uniform, and consistent body of 'sacred' law. For several decades, the early colonial government attempted to extract from Sanskrit treatises one uniform set of rules that could be applied to all Hindus as civil law. They began to appoint Brahmin pundits as interpreters of this body of law. Based upon Protestant ideas, some practices were accepted as truly religious, while others were rejected as illegitimate additions to religion. In this way the colonial legal system effectively transplanted its Christian conceptual structure on to the Hindu traditions.

Arya: In any case, it is inconceivable at this point in time to replace our existing structures with some sort of vague traditional form of government.

Leela: I am by no means suggesting that we need to extract some alleged 'Hindu beliefs' out of ancient texts. Just because I criticize the notion of a liberal secular state in India, does not mean I defend the idea of some sort of retrograde 'faith-based' state. But this does not mean that we cannot challenge the entire framework of liberal political theory so that we may work towards the creation of alternative conceptual frameworks. Since many scholars have remarked on the reasonably stable and plural society that existed in India, it must have had some successful mechanisms for co-existence between diverse groups. We need not romanticize this as some sort of pristine harmony but there is certainly a need to investigate these forms of co-existence and find out how they work. What were the sets of practices and attitudes that allowed people to co-exist?

Science has given us the heuristics to arrive at reliable theoretical knowledge about the world. Any theories that we develop on the traditional ways of living together must share the characteristic features of a scientific hypothesis. Our hypotheses must be refutable, coherent, internally consistent, and able to be continually refined. Once we gain some insight into these forms of co-existence, these can then serve as conceptual resources for developing a new political theory of pluralism that can be presented as an alternative to the liberal secular model.

Reeti: I agree that in India we have something unique that we don't see elsewhere in the world. Although there are occasional violent clashes, there is also a tendency in each of the religious or traditional groups to adopt elements from the other traditions. Certain festivals, artistic traditions and saints are shared by Hindus, Muslims and Christians. In many parts of India this kind of positive interaction lives on today.

Arya: But this type of pluralism also exists all over America and in many other parts of the West. It is not unique to India.

Leela: But the whole point of this conversation is to show how the western world continues to operate under the religious cognitive framework even when it professes to be multi-cultural. Even when people from the West directly adopt the Asian traditions, whether they practice Hinduism or Buddhism, they approach them as a form of Protestant Christianity. Our gurus in the West do the same thing, whether knowingly or not. The pluralism in Indian culture is very different. Our contemporary ignorance of the mechanisms behind this pluralist social structure is tragic, given the fact that it is in fast decline.

Arya: Well then, all I can say is that I hope we practice what we preach and truly examine the nature of Indian pluralism before making any claims about its value.

Leela: Of course we must be rigorous in our approach. But before we do anything we need to create a climate that stimulates and sustains such research projects. Rather than singing the mantras of secularism, we should strive to provide a fertile soil for innovative research on the co-existence of communities in India. We need to develop exciting new fields of study that will turn our current understanding of human beings and societies upside down. Though much work needs to be done, I am convinced that we will be able to show that the Indian traditions have a particular cognitive value that may be richer than the idea of secularism.

Arya: We are what we are today, influenced in uncountable ways by other cultures and traditions. It makes me very uncomfortable if there's even a hint of a suggestion that we are looking for some kind of 'pure' Indian culture.

Leela: Nobody's looking for a pure Indian culture that needs to be dug up from its ancient, mythical, pristine and unsullied past. We have to work within the limits set by the present. Ever since modern colonialism, western culture has presented itself as an alternate and desirable form of life to peoples from non-western cultures. But there is an asymmetry here: non-western cultures are never seen as alternatives to the western form of life, even if the West might adopt some aspects of other cultures. This indicates that western culture is seen as the 'endpoint' for non-western cultures. It is only as such do we meet each other in the world arena. However, no intellectual domain has done the kind of research that shows why western culture is the only alternative to non-western cultures. It's about time we challenged this lack of symmetry. We must challenge it not because it is western or Christian, but because it does not make sense in the Indian context.

Reeti: It does seem odd that most Hindus can relate to the idea that Hinduism is not a religion but have never bothered to question what the implications of this can be for the idea of secularism. Not only that, but I feel like there's a form of censorship in that we are not allowed to question secularism. The minute we do so we are branded as fundamentalists. As if secularism is a sacred doctrine that is immune to any genuine intellectual challenge. I find this type of secular fundamentalism to be as troubling as religious fundamentalism and would love to find a way out of this quagmire.

Leela: In the eyes of the Indian secularists, it seems unthinkable that the framework of secularism could be flawed to its very core. This demonstrates a massive failure of imagination; the sacrificing of creativity to inertia. The problems that secularism was designed to solve remain as acute as ever. States around the world continue to confront tension and conflict between communities. The only framework available for interpreting and answering such questions remains the theology of Christian liberty with its principle of the separation of the two realms. By importing these theological ideas into the social sciences we cannot claim to have produced knowledge. It is *not* science. We cannot use these ideas to study human beings, societies, or other cultures. In many instances they are completely inapplicable to other cultures.

In its arrogance, the West claims that these are universal descriptions; in our foolishness, we accept such claims as true. We carry on using these ideas as if we are being scientific and reasonable, while overlooking the increasing failure of the liberal model to produce peacefully diverse societies. What if we didn't just accept these compromises but tried to improve or resolve them? Imagine that.

CHAPTER VII

A WORLD OF DIFFERENCE

Leela: I used to naively believe that cultural difference is something that most of us would not experience, given that we had had a western education. Pretty soon I realized that I was wrong. Thus began a long journey towards trying to figure out this puzzle. What makes Indian culture different from that of the West? I began to research this issue with some vague hunches and intuitions as my reference points, without any real literature to guide me in my endeavor. This is because anthropology has still not progressed beyond disputes about definitions and silly theories about human culture. The existing tracts show no inkling of even sensing the problem let alone solving it. It's as if there is nothing to learn from different cultures other than to collect facts about them. It's one thing to experience cultural differences, but it's a task of an entirely different magnitude to say what this experience consists of or what makes it 'cultural'.

Arya: I would have thought that that would be the most interesting thing about studying other cultures – the idea that we can learn from them. I know that you have been developing a program on a comparative study of cultures for a while. How did you go about building your ideas and what do you think would be a more fruitful way to study cultural differences?

Leela: Well, we can begin by just looking at culture in an intuitive way. Basically, we encounter cultural differences in inter-individual human contacts. That is, we do not meet 'western culture' but individual Americans, Germans, etc. Neither do they see 'Indian culture' but rather they meet individual Indians.

Arya: If it is about individual encounters, how can you tell whether the difference you notice is not just a matter of a personality difference or a difference in social class? For instance, Reeti's personality and mine are just as different from each other as the personality of some of my European friends is from my own. So how can you distinguish between cultural differences, personality differences and other sorts of differences?

Leela: This really is the crux of the matter. Each individual human being is a combination of biological and social inheritance, psychological makeup, and cultural upbringing. When we meet individuals we notice all of these differences. Let's say we come across a Belgian, living in America. He loves hip hop and Indian food. He goes to the Unitarian Church, calls himself an atheist, and is a nuclear scientist. Let's say you are just his opposite in many ways and yet you become friends and get to know each other well. In your interactions with him, you notice many differences between yourself and this person. From among all these differences, which ones express his sociality, which his culturality and which his personality, and for what reasons are they that? Does this person belong to one culture or to many cultures? Are his 'personal traits' actually personal, or social, or cultural, or biological? So, to get down to the really interesting question in general terms: "What makes some difference, any difference, into a cultural difference as against, say, a social or a psychological difference?"

Reeti: I guess a proper answer to such questions can only come through a global collaborative effort where people from different cultures talk about the distinguishing features of their own cultures.

Leela: On one level, this is exactly what we need right now. But on another level, the passport of a person is strictly irrelevant to conducting such a study. It is more about building a sound scientific theory than about collecting all sorts of facts from different cultures. The insider/outsider distinction is empty when it comes to saying what cultural differences are. It does not matter who develops the theories, as long as we develop the proper conceptual tools that enable us to make a distinction between 'cultural' and 'non-cultural'. The current crop of social sciences does not meet this burden.

Reeti: But even if you develop the conceptual tools, it can only give you an insight into what it means to be Indian or Asian, or Hindu. How can it help you understand western culture, or Latin American or African cultures? Since we feel like our experiences are often trivialized and distorted the insider/outsider distinction must play some role in this feeling.

Leela: I don't see why this should necessarily be the case. Western studies on India end up trivializing their subject matter because the social sciences are not real sciences. Cultural differences cannot be understood only as differences in beliefs or as differences in practices. This has been the dominant way of describing cultures, but this is merely the way western culture experiences all cultures. In fact, this was one of the central insights in Edward Said's *Orientalism*. He showed that Orientalism had less to do with the Orient than it did with the western world. While generating descriptions of other cultures, the West made use of a vast conceptual reservoir consisting of ideas and theories about human beings, the structure of societies, the value of history, or the problem of politics. In doing so, it created and reinforced ideas about *western* man and *western* society. However, it presented these ideas as if they were true of the entire world. So by studying Orientalism we actually study western culture. It shows us what constraints operate upon western thought that result in the limited vocabulary and imagery when it comes to describing other cultures. In their descriptions of other cultures, the 'otherness' of the others disappears. The West is the great original and all other cultures are pale imitations.

Reeti: But I still don't get how you can escape from falling into the same trap. If the West is constrained by its culture, then you must be constrained by yours.

Leela: I have the advantage of having learned from their mistakes. This cognitive failure of western culture provides me with a reference point that allows me to escape the constraints of my culture, and, in doing so, to become subservient only to the dynamics of producing a scientific theory. The development of my theory will be subject to the dynamics and constraints that govern any scientific theory, and only to that.

Like many of us, I started on this project just by noticing that western scholarship on India follows certain patterns. These patterns do not make much sense to Indians even if they do to the western world. Many of us sense that something is wrong somewhere, even if most of us cannot articulate quite what it is. We feel the need to get to the bottom of this. We begin to read up on these things – some Edward Said here, some Foucault there, some literature on the Africans, or the Native Americans, and what do we find? This western way of talking is not confined to Indian culture alone but that western scholarship about all other cultures follows exactly the same pattern. So we carry on reading a bit more, from different people, from different periods in time. They say the same things, even if they use different imagery and different jargon. We now begin to get a clear picture that this is not merely an idiosyncrasy of a few writers or a fad from a particular time period. Maybe it has to do with western culture itself? At this moment in our research, we merely have an intuitive idea of what western culture is, so we read a bit more, say, what the Islamic rulers and writers said about our traditions. We see that they said more or less the same things. So while it could be something western, yet this might have something to do with what religion is. Then we read and reflect on what Indians said about Christianity and Islam and we notice that they did not say similar things at all. Two possibilities open up: either our 'religions' are special, or they might not be religions at all. Then we start reading about religion and think some more. This process continues until we are able to formulate a tractable problem and come up with a testable hypothesis. Notice that we did not embark on any fact-finding mission; nor are we inducing anything by first collecting trillions upon trillions of facts. We are doing research that is hypothesis-driven and that is capable of being tested at every step. But what was the starting point? Just the feeling that something is wrong (cognitively wrong, that is) with the way Indian culture has been depicted by the West. Of course, it is not all smooth sailing; there are many false starts, blind alleys, or an inability to see the obvious at times. But this is the process of all scientific enquiries and all theory building. This has nothing to do with a person's ethnicity or passport.

Reeti: You say repeatedly that the study of cultures must go beyond looking at beliefs and practices. I'm having a hard time imagining what other ways there might be of distinguishing one culture from another.

Leela: I can sketch the outlines of my theory on cultural difference to give you an idea of an alternate way of going about this task. It involves a study of human cultures structurally, from the point of view of their learning processes. It then relates the configuration of the various different learning processes to the way people in these cultures go about in the world.

Reeti: You're going to have to break that down for me, I'm afraid.

Leela: There are many different kinds of learning processes in a culture – the kind that enables you to write poetry, to do science, build architecture, create music and dance, relate to people, and so on. Although there are many different learning processes in each culture, one learning process dominates while others are subordinated. That is to say, something or the other coordinates the many different kinds of learning processes present in each culture. This 'something' I call a configuration of learning. Through the coordination of different kinds of learning processes, a configuration of learning slowly comes into being. This configuration of learning, where a particular learning process is dominant while others are subordinate gives rise to a specific culture because of its unique configuration.

Reeti: I don't think I understand. How does some learning process come to dominate or what brings this about, for example?

Leela: It is my suggestion that in the West, a fundamental model of order brings about a configuration of learning. This root model is religion which configures learning processes by structuring the experience of the world in a particular way. Typically, this specific way of learning involves 'knowing about'. It produces a culture-specific knowledge, namely, theoretical knowledge, that we call the sciences.

Arya: Okay, let's take this a step at a time. What exactly does it signify when you say 'knowing about'?

Leela: It is the idea that to go about in the world you need to have knowledge about the world. This idea is structured by religion where knowing what there is in the world is a way of trying to decipher God's will as it is expressed in the world. The intellectual and practical energies of this culture are focused on discovering these regularities in nature. Actions in the world are 'proper' insofar as 'knowledge about' an action guides the actions. To be a friend or a father, one must know what it is to be a friend or a father; to build a good society, one must first know what a good society is; to build human relationships, one must know what they are. Religion serves as a basic model for all types of learning in the West and inspires all types of explanations, including scientific explanations. Reason plays an important role in this process from beginning to end since the fundamental belief is that God made the world for a reason. Going-about in the world involves rational deliberation based on rational criteria, and actions are an execution of these rational decisions.

Reeti: I suppose this would be another reason why people from the West are compelled to tie practices to beliefs.

Leela: That's right. In such a culture, human actions are described according to their intentional states, or as an expression of beliefs, based on which human beings make choices. Because human actions are thought to be expressions of beliefs, knowledge about other cultures means having knowledge about the beliefs of these cultures. In other words, this culture-specific way of learning is also expressed in the way this culture seeks to understand other cultures.

The gradual emergence of religion as the root model of order is, among other things, what made the West into a culture. Religion developed a way of learning through which science could emerge by making the will of the Sovereign constant, and His works trustworthy, in an absolutely perfect way. It severed the link that had tied the sciences to an elite social group, thereby generalizing the attitude required for the growth of the sciences. Now the sciences could develop, expand, and flourish in the cognitive soil prepared for them.

Reeti: Considering that the whole world has accepted science and technology with open arms, does this then mean that their unique learning configurations, whatever they may be, are now altered? Indians, for example, are excellent in science, so have we now somehow reconfigured our learning processes?

Leela: It's irrelevant to my hypothesis whether Indians are good at science or Americans are good at yoga. Anyone can learn to solve an equation or to stand on their head. Rather, it is about the attitude that generates these disciplines in the first place. When we say, for instance, that we need to learn science from the West, this does not mean that we need to learn some specific scientific formula from the West. I am looking at the sciences from a different level of abstraction. I am suggesting that there is a *way of going about* in the world that we need to learn from the West. My hypothesis about science and religion is pitched at this level of abstraction. I try to answer the following question: in which way is the growth of the sciences a cultural phenomenon? How the Indians learn whatever they learn is in accordance with their own ways of going about in the world. The Indian configuration of learning determines how they learn whatever they learn.

Reeti: But what is the Indian configuration of learning then? And what brings it about?

Leela: If we look at configurations of learning as cultural answers to the question 'how to live', one way of answering this question, as we just saw, is to find out what there is in the world. Another answer can be derived by finding out *how to go about* in the world. We can look at both the question and the answer in performative terms. In this case, a practical or performative learning process dominates the configuration of learning. As a culturally-specific way of learning, it also gives identity to a culture. Its way of going-about solves the problem of 'how to live' not by building a worldview but by developing an ability to try to live the best one can. Since the dominant unit of teaching in such a culture does not impart knowledge about the world, such units of knowledge cannot be considered explanatory in nature. Moreover, its dominant mode of learning is deeply connected to practices. That is, goings-about in the world must themselves be experienced in performative terms.

Reeti: And what generates this type of learning process?

Leela: In India, it is ritual that brings about a culturally-specific way of going about in the world. Ritual is a structured set of generic actions that can be described as non-intentional, agent-less, and goal-less. Learning to do rituals is performative and the way in which members of this culture go about in the world is itself recognizably ritualized.

Reeti: Wait, let's back up a little. I'm having trouble digesting the part about non-intentional, agent-less, and goal-less actions. Most rituals do have some underlying purpose. Only from a scientific perspective could you possibly say that rituals are meaningless, but from the perspective of tradition this is irrelevant. Rituals, I think, do embody meaning.

Leela: Rituals are what they are due to their structure. What is important about ritual is how to do it rather than its meaning. Our contemporary obsession with meaning and symbolism comes from our acceptance of ideas that have been handed down to us from the religious cultures. Religious cultures do believe that actions are differentiated according to the intentional states of an actor. That is, actions are what an *actor* does; what he hopes, desires, or anticipates to achieve thereby. On this view, minimally we need at least two things to identify an action – an actor and their intentions. This is because in a learning configuration structured by religion, actions are supposed to be expressions of belief-states; and because belief-states are always *someone's* belief states, we need an actor. By contrast, in the ritual-based configuration of learning, this is not the case. That is why rituals are agent-less and goal-less or meaningless.

Arya: Is it because we mechanically go about the motions, or repeat mantras?

Leela: I don't think it will do to fall back on the common description of rituals within the West which is to say that they are mechanical and repetitive. They seem mechanical because it appears difficult to specify them in terms of intentional states. Remember, in the common-sense psychology of the West, even opening a window is seen as an intentional act. In exactly the same intentional psychology, rituals appear mechanical and it is difficult to fit them under an intentional description. The point or the goal of ritual does not appear to be evident. Bear in mind that we are not discussing human actions as they are conceptualized in the western configuration of learning. We are trying to think about another configuration of learning which structures human goings-about differently. People think, dream, and hope in every culture. People reason everywhere too. One way to talk about the relation between thought and action is to say that 'actions are intentional'. However, there are other ways of expressing the relation between action and thought, including one where thought or reason merely limits action.

Reeti: Okay, I get the part about religion and intentionality. But I cannot for the life of me grasp what you're trying to convey about non-intentional and agent-less actions. I'm convinced that we do rituals for a reason. Moreover, rituals function to reduce anxiety, or they can act as a cementing bond within the community. Sometimes they are done to celebrate or solemnize occasions. I don't see how you can justify characterizing them as goal-less, meaningless and purposeless.

Leela: Let me see how I can describe this better. Consider, say, a simple everyday ritual like the *sandhya vandanam* and let's look at two ways of describing it. One way goes deep into which *mudras* are used in this ritual and what the *mudras* mean; it analyzes the *pranayama* that accompanies the ritual; it goes into what the *Gayatri* mantra means; and so on. At the other extreme is an ordinary individual who performs all the prescribed actions without knowing what any of them mean. When asked, one of them tells us about his in-depth research and the other simply says: "I don't know what any of this means. I just perform the ritual because I have been taught to perform it this particular way." The question then becomes: Which one of these claims is a true description of what rituals are? Unless you make a meta assumption about whether rituals ought to have a meaning, you cannot privilege one story above the other. Now consider a third person who says none of these actions mean anything at all. When all three perform the same ritual, is it possible to say of any one of them that they are not doing the *sandhya vandanam*? Let's say the three have a debate. The third one says of the first interpretation: "I don't deny that you can interpret the ritual that way, or some other way. But that is how *you* interpret it. That need not be the only true interpretation. In fact, my Guru told me that a truly enlightened person does all these rituals without ascribing any meaning to them. The enlightened person knows that it is not *they* that are performing any of these actions; they do it without any goal or purpose in mind. Therefore, the real meaning of this ritual is what it is to the enlightened person: it means nothing." Would our traditions allow us to say that this claim is false? Our traditions allow us to say that each of these claims is true. The 'truth' of the claim is relativized to the person performing the ritual. To put it in logical terms, we have the following situation: something has meaning (this is true); there is no awareness of any meaning (this is true); the same thing has no meaning (this is true). The logical conclusion? This thing is indifferent to meaning-ascription. The 'truth value' of the ritual does not change as the 'meaning' of that ritual changes. Therefore, it does not make sense to talk about rituals in terms of the meanings they allegedly embody.

Reeti: But why then do I have this gut feeling that rituals have meaning? You cannot just ignore the way most people feel but must be able to account for this feeling as well. As you yourself said, any good theory must be able to account for the way people experience the situation.

Leela: Okay, let's take the chanting of mantras, for instance. In some sense, our Indian commonsense preserves the insight that such things have meaning by ascribing a sense of efficacy to mantras, whether the performer is aware or ignorant of the meaning of the mantras. This insight does not mean that the mantras have some magical potency (even though this is how our folk psychology puts it), but that they are indifferent to meanings. They just work, says our commonsense. You say that it is your gut feeling that rituals are not meaningless. My only answer is that it is not any gut feeling at all but your westernized consciousness that speaks here. This consciousness makes certain meta assumptions about human actions and regards human beings who perform meaningless actions as insane. You must have noticed, too, that people from the West who practice the eastern traditions almost always inquire about the meaning of a mantra. This is not usually the case with Indians who are not concerned about the meaning so much as the performative aspects of a mantra, such as how often to repeat it, when the best time to do so is, how to pronounce it correctly, and so on.

Arya: I'm sorry, but I'm having a hard time accepting this. Not that I ever do rituals, but why would anyone bother to do them at all if not for a reason? Why participate in a tradition unless there's a reason?

Leela: If you're looking for an explanation for the continuation of a tradition where the explanation seeks a foundation in reason then you are bound to fail in your attempt. Tradition merely transmits the practical knowledge of living together. This is why philosophers, especially during the Roman Empire, strenuously argued against having to found traditional practices on rational arguments. Their argument was that it was neither necessary nor possible to base practices on theoretical arguments. It was not necessary because practical knowledge itself was knowledge, and human practices do not require a foundation in reason. It was not possible, because the kind of certainty one falsely attributed to reason was illusory. Actions need not be guided by anything other than tradition and custom, which are themselves a species of knowledge, transmitted from generation to generation.

Reeti: Can we say that doing what our ancestors did plays the same role in the Indian traditions that faith does in religion? In a way we can say that we 'believe' that we must continue our traditions and that is the reason we do them.

Leela: Let's try and look at it another way. When someone justifies their practices by referring to a set of beliefs, it means that they are providing a logically derived conclusion based on a set of premises. There is, however, another way of looking at the notion of 'justification'. We can justify an action by pointing to some other action. In this case, 'justification' refers to some kind of a relation between actions, and not between beliefs. Even though it might not be clear at this moment what kind of a relation should exist between two actions such that one action justifies another, the point is that such a justification is also possible. So I would say that indeed one can justify the continuation of a tradition without having the belief that one must continue the tradition. From the philosophical perspective, one of the problems we need to solve is about the relation between beliefs and actions. Are actions caused by beliefs, or based on beliefs (in the sense of being reasons for an action)? I am convinced that such 'beliefs' about actions are merely a way of talking about actions and not their cause.

Arya: But then what about the various reform movements that provide rational grounds for discontinuing certain practices? This can only be the case if those practices were founded on some sort of reason to start with.

Leela: I am not claiming that reason cannot provide the grounds for starting, stopping or modifying a practice. If I did, that would just make me a simple-minded relativist who believes that every practice is alright just because it is a traditional practice. In fact, one of the main tasks of reason is precisely to limit, constrain and guide our actions. But in the Indian traditions the role of reason is from the outside, so to speak. Unlike Christianity, which attributes reasons or beliefs as a *foundation* for practices, this is not so in the practice of the pagan traditions. What Christianity did, something that Judaism had done much earlier, was to try to absorb practical knowledge into the theoretical and to see human activity as the execution of a plan. When theologians began to conceptualize human action, the nature of God's actions was the contrasting model, because we are made in His image. As we saw, religion tells us that God's will and God's actions coincide perfectly with each other. Therefore, the central problem in the Christian understanding of human action became the question about the relation between our intentions and our actions. The conviction is that somehow our actions must embody reasons. However, the reality is that this cannot happen. It does not even make sense to pose such questions regarding human action. This unsolvable question propels the social sciences into investigations about the nature of human action and continues to perpetuate the belief that actions are based on reason.

Reeti: But surely the fact that I go to work every day counts as an action that is the very embodiment of reason?

Leela: If you begin to examine this notion in some detail you may change your mind about what you just said. Let's say some hypothetical person decides to find a well-paying job instead of pursuing their dream of becoming an artist or a writer. We tend to describe this as a choice based on reasons. But when we consider the process by which people make such decisions, it is impossible to say what counts as the real reason. They will have considered a set of reasons for both of their choices. Both sets of reasons are just as reasonable since there are as many convincing reasons for one choice as there are for the other. Naturally, once the decision has been made, they will start invoking one set of reasons to justify their decision as the rational one. If they go for the well-paying job, they will invoke one set of reasons, and if they decide to become an artist, they will invoke the other set of reasons. This suggests that reason plays a role other than that of bringing forth the action. Let's add another factor to this scenario to highlight my point. Let's say they then discover that they are about to have a baby. Suddenly the reasons for finding a well-paying job begin to sound much more cogent, and the reasons for pursuing their artistic dreams begin to sound trivial. Now, instead of looking at this as something that is based on reason, it could just as well be described as a situation where one action brings forth another action. That is to say, there is a cycle of actions that leads to the ultimate action of finding a proper job. From this perspective, what we need to try and explain is this: what are the principles that allow one action to justify another action. Here it is not the case that we need to look for a reason or belief or intention that justifies an action.

Arya: All right, if we go by this perspective then we have to rule out reason as a foundation for beliefs or actions. But on top of this, you want to rule out all intentional states such as desire and hope. So are we then supposed to look at it from the perspective of things like 'motivation', 'need', or 'function'? I feel like anything is preferable to conceding to the proposition that actions are inherently meaningless.

Leela: Our understanding of words such as 'motivation' is even more elusive than our understanding of reason. For instance, is motivation something other than a psychological or biological need expressed in the language of reasons or is there something called 'motivation' that is different from needs? Current social science research on the relation between motives and actions leaves most such questions unanswered. Can people know their own motives? Is there a relation between conscious and unconscious motives? Do motives change? How do we know the real motive? There are no commonly accepted answers to such questions.

In any case, why does an action stand in need of justification by something else? Imagine a similar question being raised with respect to human thinking. Do we think because there is a reason for thinking, or because there is a need for thinking or because there is a motivation to think? Any general answer you could give to these questions is equally applicable to action. We think because we cannot not think; we act because we cannot not act. Action does not need justification any more than thinking does.

Arya: Okay, I give up. But at least all of the digging into causes and reasons by the western religious configuration brought forth the natural sciences. If a ritualistically-oriented society is non-intentional and goal-less, how does it sustain itself? If beliefs and reasons have little do to with how people go about in the world and if 'knowing about' or theoretical knowledge is not considered important, then there must be some other form of knowledge that comes about.

Leela: The kind of knowledge generated by ritual is performative knowledge or 'knowing how'. It is the knowledge involved in building and sustaining human groups and societies. What ritual does is to develop this ability further. More broadly put, the domain of performative knowledge is the social environment. If performative knowledge is dominant in a culture, the social environment will exhibit an extraordinary degree of stability, cohesion, complexity and dynamism. Individual members should be able to reproduce such an environment without knowing the rules of its reproduction.

Arya: Doesn't religion too serve a cohesive function? Since we are talking about cultural differences, what is the difference in the way this functions in different cultures?

Leela: Empirical histories of religions in fact show that religion divides communities; it does not unite them. Neither can we say that ritual unites communities because ritual is mostly done individually at home, and in any case, it is impossible to identify any ritual practice that is common to Indians. Performative knowledge plays a role in the creation and reproduction of societies both in the East and in the West. My point is that this is not directly the result of either religion or ritual. Rather, it is because ritual generates a configuration of learning whose *dominant* learning process builds societies. Religion generates another configuration of learning whose *subordinate* learning process builds societies.

Arya: What are the other characteristic features of a culture shaped by ritual?

Leela: Such cultures would be dominated by mimetic learning which is what would shape the spheres of morality, law, social organization, and human interaction. Practical knowledge is cumulative perhaps to a greater degree than knowledge in the theoretical sphere. The form of social organization in India is one such cumulative result. No Indian could tell you what the principles of social organization among the various *jatis* (ethnic groups) are, yet it reproduces itself because there is knowledge available to reproduce it. There are no theories to be found within the Indian traditions about how this social organization sustains itself. Yet there appears to be an enormous repertoire of do's and don'ts, even in the absence of social institutions or centralized authorities to enforce them. Clearly this means that there is some kind of knowledge present in this society and that it is available to its members. Each member of such a form of life must have access to this knowledge otherwise there would be no continuity between generations and hence no culture either. Given that Indian society has some such thing called culture and some kind of a history, then the question is: If knowledge 'about' these practices is not what there is, what other kind of knowledge is it? How is such knowledge transmitted through generations? How do individuals learn it? How does this enable them to sustain a very complex form of social interaction?

Reeti: It is rather odd, isn't it, that people have been studying caste and *jatis* in India for centuries, yet none of these studies has been able to answer such questions.

Leela: That's because we cannot use the conceptual tools of western culture to try and understand Indian culture. The way I suggest tackles the problem from the perspective of 'action knowledge'. It is not knowledge about actions; neither is it the same as acquiring some skill or the other. This is a species of knowledge that is distinct from theoretical knowledge and it is acquired by learning through exemplars. Although the western social sciences do study action, there has been no serious attempt to relate the kind of knowledge that actions generate to cultural studies. The underlying assumption is that the problems they study are the same across cultures. This is the deep and fundamental belief that grounds the intuitions of western culture. To the members of this culture, it appears obvious that human action exhibits some typical, species-specific properties such as being intentional, goal-directed, or rational. But there are other ways of acting and other ways of going about in the world. We need to develop a more adequate notion of action-knowledge by looking at how it functions across different cultures. Perhaps we will find that such cultures will be as preoccupied with rituals as western culture is preoccupied with religion. It is my belief that Asia is one such culture.

Reeti: Are you saying that there is something that can be called 'Asian culture' the way we can speak of western culture?

Leela: I think it would be very interesting to study if there is some sort of structural similarity between the different traditions spread across Asia. It seems plausible when we consider that the traditions we call 'Hinduism' and 'Buddhism' migrated so easily across the whole of Asia. Remember this happened without any kind of centralized authority (military, political, economic or religious) to enforce it. It would be quite plausible to hypothesize that there must be something fundamentally similar between the different Asian cultures that make them into Asian culture. It could be that the strategy of social interaction is the same within these cultures. That is, one could speak in terms of the western way of going about and the Asian way of going about. If only we could isolate these strategies of social interaction, we would have the necessary formal tools to start investigating this!

Reeti: I think I too have noticed some similarities between people from different Asian cultures. When I had room-mates, I noticed that the Asians and the Africans tended to share things more, while the westerners were more self-sufficient. In any case, they certainly hesitated to ask to borrow something even if they were happy to lend. A sense of sharing did not seem to come so naturally to them as it did to the rest of us.

Leela: This claim is an excellent example of what happens when we try to account for the differences between cultures without developing a proper theory of cultural difference. Many of us have had similar experiences like your room-mate experience. We notice the fact that people in India share things a lot more while people in the West seem to live in their own bubbles even when they live together. Our intuition tells us this has something to do with the cultural difference between India and the West. So far, so good. But when we leap to the next step by 'explaining' this as individualistic or community-oriented behavior we run into problems. First of all, it does not give us any insight into our experience of the differences between India and the West. Instead of allowing us to reflect on this experience, such 'explanations' stop all further reflection. It gives us the illusion that we have explained something while all we have done is to slap some labels on to things we notice.

One way to test whether we have really explained something is to see whether you could just as easily reverse this labeling. What if we were to pick out another set of facts about India and the West? Let's look at the way in which the Indian traditions say that people with different aptitudes and inclinations find happiness through different routes and this can be called 'individualistic', while Christianity's claim that all should follow Christ to attain salvation can be called 'collectivistic'. When we can switch the labels this easily, it means that they lack cognitive value. Attempts to elaborate on such labels generally appeal to the belief systems of the two cultures. They say things like "in the worldview of the modern West, individual autonomy is supreme, while Indians believe that the individual is always subordinate to the community." This is the standard way of conceptualizing cultural differences. Cultures are seen to differ insofar as they have different beliefs about the world. This way of thinking does not lead us anywhere in terms of making sense of the cultural difference that we noticed.

Reeti: How, then, could we understand our room-mate experiences and find out what is cultural about these differences?

Leela: As I said, we need to develop sound theories that move beyond the constraints of seeing cultural differences as differences in beliefs. To do so, however, we need to start at a very high level of abstraction. This has been my approach where I characterize cultural differences as configurations of different kinds of learning processes. These learning configurations structure our attitudes and determine how we go about in the world. This hypothesis needs to be more fully developed and this takes years of research. This may sound disappointing at first but I am convinced that this approach will prove to be more fruitful compared to the sterile theories from the social sciences which do not go beyond definitions and fixations on beliefs. There are many more kinds of learning processes than the theoretical and the performative alone (for example, the kinds that produce poetry, architecture, music or dance), and many more possible configurations of these various learning processes. In principle, one could study the African cultures as particular configurations of learning and theorize about the cultural differences between Africa and Asia caused by the dominance of different kinds of learning processes. So you see, there is the potential to study cultures as being different from each other in different ways, rather than all cultures being variants of western culture.

Reeti: But do we really need to develop a theory before we can begin to understand something? This sounds unnecessarily restrictive.

Leela: Of course we don't need to have a theory before we can understand something. But if we really understand something we can explain it by developing a sound theory. Otherwise, anyone can come up with *ad hoc* reasons or explanations based on their pet beliefs and call it a theory. I don't have any fetish about theories, and, in fact, allow for all kinds of knowledge other than theoretical knowledge. However, any 'theory' that makes an entire culture sound like a collection of idiots is implausible. This is precisely what you get when you approach cultural studies the way the western social sciences do. The western approach is not even useful in studying its own culture. A viable hypothesis about the Christian West should be able to explain why geniuses like Thomas Aquinas were fascinated by questions about how many angels can fit on the head of a pin. Even Newton, one of the greatest geniuses of all time, was busy trying to decipher God's world. Dismissive sneers about this attitude will not do. We can easily make fun of theologians as fools who were obsessed by trivial questions. But this means that we have failed to understand their religion and their culture. The current crop of atheistic scholars is an example of this failing. They treat the Bible as if it is a mere book, conveniently overlooking the fact that religion includes what it says about itself. The religious account tells us that the Bible is the word of God. You cannot just bracket away this claim and still study the Bible to understand Christianity as a religion. If you do, then the object of your study is no longer religion but literature, and that is not what has structured western thinking. These atheists merely succeed in demonstrating that all non-scientific disciplines are populated by dim-wits while the bright light of the Enlightenment illumines the rest of them. But it is hard to take their 'Enlightenment' seriously when you consider that colonialism, the Holocaust, the genocide of the Native Americans, and the pogroms under the socialist regimes are all post-Enlightenment events. For all practical purposes, their 'enlightened' worldview does not fare any better when juxtaposed with the religious atrocities that they rail against.

Reeti: Speaking of worldviews, you keep insisting that Indians do not have worldviews and that their actions are guided by other actions or imitations of actions. But wouldn't you have to agree that our ideas of karma and reincarnation form our worldview? I understand that these ideas have more to do with our folk psychology and are not a part of our intellectual traditions, but they can be characterized as worldviews nevertheless.

Leela: Again, this is a typically western way of posing such questions: why do Indians have the worldview they have? Why do they talk in terms of the *atman* or karma? These are seen as different beliefs, belonging to different worldviews, but in fact such questions exhibit the conceptual weakness of western culture in such matters. To appreciate this as a conceptual weakness, look at what Christianity did. It imagined the 'others' to be variants of itself. If indeed God came to the Arabian Desert several times and gave religion to a people, "why did God do so" is a question that cannot be answered. Its exact correlate is our inability to answer the question why different cultures have different 'worldviews.' The West sees the differences between cultures only in its terms, as having another (different) worldview. It cannot conceptualize things in any other way. It channels all its intellectual energies towards discovering order buried underneath a postulated chaos and produces philosophers, theologians, and scientists. The idea is that given a good set of principles, good rules, and good statutes, the emergence of a good society and good human beings will be logical consequences. But when you look at the real world, this idea does not hold up. Theories grow rich and sophisticated, whereas daily life becomes barren and poor. Contrast this with Indian culture. All its intellectual energies went towards creating, sustain-

ing, and continuously modifying a social or practical order. Theoretical disquisitions about some imagined order were neither essential nor much encouraged. A peculiar kind of theoretical poverty emerged as a result.
And when we needed it most, we simply did not have
the theoretical apparatus to respond in any meaningful
way to the assault on our culture and traditions.

Reeti: But if India indeed does not have religions or
worldviews, then in what other terms can we explain the
similarity between, say, *Bhakti* and the characteristi-
cally religious feeling in the West?

Leela: The first point to consider is that merely noting a similarity between two entities does not tell us much. It is
always possible to draw a similarity relationship between any two objects in the world in one way or another. I could say that a monkey is similar to my laptop
because they both contain carbon. This is not a particularly interesting observation. Things can have something in common in one particular description of the
world and not in another. A human being can be studied
at the cellular level, at the biological level, at the sociological level, at the political level, and in many other
ways. They can have similarities in some fields and
nothing in common in others. In this way, when looked
at from the religious perspective, there is nothing in
common between, say, Asia and the West.

The presence of elements in cultures, which resemble
each other very closely, does not tell us much in and by
itself. These elements could be the products of entirely
different processes. We can either focus on these elements, or study the structure. That is, we can either regard culture as a set of elements, or we can see it as a
structured way of going about in the world. The typical
way to study cultures so far has been to focus on the
elements. It has not been particularly fruitful in providing any insight into cultural differences. That is why it

is better not to look at elements within a culture, but to look instead at how people go about in the world.

Reeti: Okay, I think I can see what you're getting at. We experience different cultural patterns in different parts of the world. While it may be helpful to study the West in terms of religion, it does not yield any knowledge to study India through the same framework.

Leela: If we have to get out of this quandary, we need to do something radical with respect to what counts as knowledge and what does not in the field of cultural difference. My response has been to accept the best criteria of rationality and scientificity that the study of the *natural sciences* has brought forth. One of the crucial tests for evaluating the claims about any culture, including Indian culture, is the extent to which a theory makes sense of the experience of Indians without denying, distorting, or transforming those experiences. So far I have been able to make better sense of what unites Indians without using the word 'Hinduism' or any of its dominant meanings. I am approaching this problem by trying to make sense of things such as 'experiential knowledge', or 'practical' or 'performative knowledge' to build a testable hypothesis about Indian culture. No doubt we will need to coin more new words. Let us see where my search takes me. I know where the search of the last three hundred years has led and I have no intention of going there.

Arya: But people have objected that science is also just a human construct. Besides it is reductive in nature and cannot make sense of individual experience without gross generalizations.

Leela: Ever notice that it's only people from the western world who complain that science is merely a human construct? Naturally they are inclined to think along these lines because unlike their religion which has been gifted straight from God, science is merely human. For the rest of us who are content to deal with the merely human, science is the best model we have right now if we want to try and understand or explain things. People have this feeling that scientific explanations, with their emphasis on rationality and objectivity, are reductive in nature. I don't agree at all. If you want to enjoy an autumn sunset you don't open Feynman's Lectures on Physics; you go elsewhere. Science is not meant to provide you with the ability to experience a beautiful sunset, not does it claim to do so.

Theories in the natural sciences are not reductive in the sense that they do not reduce the beauty of a sunset to the motion of the earth around the sun even if they are able to explain the sunrise and sunset. The current crop of social sciences does precisely this. While seeming to be about human beings, their psychologies, their societies and their cultures, the tales they spin reflect the same monochromatic dullness. The social sciences seem to be aware of this shortcoming and the dominant explanation for this sad state of affairs is that without 'reducing' human beings into objects, it is not possible to do science. We're supposed to live with the fact that we have silly sociological theories and stupid psychological ones, because it is in the nature of human beings to defy being objectified and science cannot work any other way. This is how western culture has been studying human beings, their societies, and their cultures all this while. There is nothing remotely scientific about either this venture or its results. The limits of western culture have become the limits of the extent to which we can understand human beings and their societies. This is not a simple expression of racism, western superiority or Orientalism. Rather, it has to do with what western culture is, what its social sciences are, what Christianity is, and what the relation between all these things is. The reduction occurs not because of objective and scientific explanations, but because of secularized theological claims.

Reeti: It's unfortunate that our knowledge of the whole world comes just from the way the West has studied it. We have no idea what the world would look like if we looked at it our way.

Leela: This is the agenda for the future and it must begin with a decolonization of the social sciences. This must be a collective global effort of intellectuals across the world. This is not meant to indicate an 'us' and 'them' opposition or a 'clash of civilizations'. This opposition does exist today, and it can serve as our point of departure. From the point of view of a comparative study of cultures, Orientalism can be seen to be the *western* way of looking at the world. Let the Africans contribute their ways of looking at the world, the Asians theirs, the Latin Americans theirs, and so on. In this way we can have alternative viewpoints rather than the western way which we are supposed to believe is the only way of looking at the world. Each way of life has approached and solved the problem of human flourishing in different ways. Now we must devise reasonable criteria to find out which solutions to the specific problems of human flourishing are better than others.

Reeti: Can you give us a sketch of what it would be like to have an Indian perspective on the Indian traditions in general? I know you have already spoken about our sense of self, the ethical domain, non-normative thinking, and such. But is there an over-arching way in which we can describe the Indian traditions that includes all of these elements?

Arya: Yes, I too would be interested in getting an idea on how we can speak for the Indian traditions in ways other than what is dished out in the standard textbooks. But right now it's time to go enjoy the autumn sunset. Maybe we can delve into this tomorrow?

CHAPTER VIII

NOT BY ONE AVENUE ALONE

Leela: If I were to sum up the nature of the Indian (or Asian) traditions in one sentence as it relates to the goal of human life, here is how I would do it: Given that we are born, how can we be happy, that is to say, how can we experience *ananda*? Our traditions assure us that every human being can be happy. There are no qualifications to being happy; you can be rich or poor; stupid or intelligent; literate or illiterate; man or woman. The only requirement is that you have to try to be happy; and this endeavor forces us to reflect on experience. That is why our traditions keep throwing up gurus (even if they do take the form of some of our contemporary crop).

Reeti: I thought the goal of the Indian traditions was to attain enlightenment. Isn't happiness a sort of a lesser goal? *Ananda* is not the same as *moksha,* and usually we speak of *moksha* or *nirvana* as the highest goal.

Leela: I don't think so. The idea is to experience *ananda* as a continuous state. To attain this state you need to come to an understanding of the nature of the Self (or agency, or intentionality), which is what is meant by *moksha.*

Reeti: Are the Self, and agency and intentionality different things or the same thing? It's funny that although I'm very comfortable with the practices, I have a hard time making sense of these things when we talk about them.

Leela: No wonder our traditions make so much use of analogies, koans, and other forms of *yukti* in trying to understand such things. Consider my favorite example of the everyday phenomenon of sunrise and sunset. We see the movement of the sun on the horizon, and for a very long period of time people thought that this is the way reality is. They believed that the sun moves around the earth. With Galileo, two things happened. First, he argued that it is the earth that moves around the sun, and second, he showed us why we are compelled to see it as if the sun moves around the earth. Because of this, a distinction became necessary: the movement of the sun around the earth was now merely a phenomenon, whereas the movement of the earth around the sun was the real truth. What we previously thought of as reality became downgraded to mere appearance and something we had no idea of until then became the reality underlying this appearance. So we have three notions: the appearance, the underlying reality, and a Reality that unites the appearance with the underlying reality. Let's call them reality-1, reality-2 and reality-3. Notice, though, that this demotion of what was once considered to be reality is acceptable only because Galileo *proves* it. He explains not only what we see, but tells us why our perception is wrong and, more importantly, tells us why we are compelled to perceive it the way we do.

Reeti: Okay, but what exactly is the analogy?

Leela: Consider now another everyday phenomenon that suggests that human beings are intentional. That is, each one of us experiences ourselves as a being that wishes, dreams, hopes, desires, fears, sets up projects, and pursues ambitions. In short, it is our everyday experience that we are intentional agents. All of Semitic theology, most of western philosophy, most of western psychology, and all of our commonsense assume the truth of this experience. Some within the western intellectual traditions have found it fit to challenge this. They are called reductionists, in the sense that they reduce consciousness to brain activity. They believe that human beings are not intentional agents and that a future scientific psychology will be able to show that our current psychological theories that attribute intentional states to human beings are false. However, the problem is that by reading these scientific explanations we do not stop dreaming, hoping, desiring, or acting like moral agents. They do not tell us why, if we are under the illusion that we are intentional creatures, we are compelled to live with this illusion, or where it comes from, and how it reproduces itself. These theories blandly assure us that we are all deluded, and no more than that. Nobody would have taken Galileo's theory seriously if he had merely asserted that we are deluded in observing the movement of the sun across the sky. The same goes with respect to these reductionist theories. If they have to be taken seriously, they must tell us not merely where this illusion of being an intentional creature comes from, but, more importantly, whether and how we can be rid of this illusion. Because being an intentional creature is experiential in nature, any explanation that claims the contrary should help us experience the illusory nature of intentionality as well.

Reeti: I see. This is where the Asian traditions step in!

Leela: Indeed. They fulfill precisely this condition. They do not merely tell us where the illusion of being an intentional agent comes from, but help us experience its illusory nature as well. Because of this, the reality that we are intentional creatures is degraded to the level of appearance (or reality-1). That we are not intentional creatures is the underlying reality (or reality-2). The ultimate Reality (or reality-3) unifies the appearance with the underlying reality. There is nothing mystical or esoteric about this. These are sciences that study some aspects of the kind of creatures we human beings are.

Reeti: But then why does practically everyone in the world, across all cultures, come to have the same set of commonsense beliefs about who they are or what they are? I mean, why is it that more or less every human being thinks that the 'I' belongs to the body, or the mind, or our status, wealth, health, hopes and desires?

Leela: I think that this is an evolutionary inheritance. I also believe that this is the *avidya* or *maya* that our traditions speak of that gets in the way of enlightenment. The goal of most of the Indian traditions is to break this pattern that gets in the way of happiness. Our experience is structured by *avidya* in the sense that it generates a fundamental cognitive scheme or a narrative about this 'I', such as "my father", "my house", "I am angry", "I like this", or "I think I am right". This cognitive scheme structures our everyday experience of just about everything. What many of our traditions do, is to modify this experience by showing that the "I" is not in the experience itself but in the story that structures the experience. What we do all the time as human beings is to confuse the structure of the cognitive scheme with the structure of experience. The Indian traditions try to detach experience from the cognitive scheme built up around this "I". A huge amount of scientific research will have to be done before we can state in contemporary terminology what human experience is, how exactly human experience is structured by cognitive schemes, whether or not all human experience is structured in this way, or how we switch from one cognitive scheme to the other.

Arya: You speak of the structure of experience and also of structured experience. What is this structure that you speak of in both cases? Does it actually exist outside the realm of theorizing about it?

Leela: There are indeed two separate issues here. We need some kind of structure to be able to experience things. The "I" is one such structure. If we did not have any structure to help us focus our attention or to link new information with old, we might not be able to experience anything. Experience too is structured. Would we 'fall in love' if nobody had ever invented this expression? I don't see how it is possible to look for experiences without structure when it is structure which makes experiences possible in the first place.

Reeti: Can we go back to the basics for a minute? What is experience, or the structure of experience?

Leela: All the Indian traditions have been busy answering this question. But both posing this question and answering it are themselves experiential. For instance, according to some traditions, the structures-in-experience are not given in the experience itself. The description of the experience provides a sense of permanence because these descriptions create structures. That is why the notion of 'transience' is so powerful. The impermanence and transience of experience has to do with the realization that there are no structures like the self, specific emotions, and so on. But that does not mean that these traditions say that our experience of a tree, or a stone or a car is illusory. Rather, accessing the truth that there is no structure in such an experience constitutes enlightenment, according to these traditions.

Arya: But I thought that the basic insight is indeed supposed to be that everything is an illusion.

Leela: We need to clarify many notions before we approach the notion of experience, if we want to talk intelligibly. Otherwise, we will just keep repeating the foolish claims of generations of Indologists and specialists in the study of Indian 'religions' that, for example, the *advaitic* tradition claims that the world is an illusion. In the hands of the Indologists, the *advaitins* are made to say such foolish things as 'there is no difference between my experience of having my arm chopped off and my experience of drinking water when I am thirsty'. How does one distinguish between the 'illusion' of having an arm chopped off and the 'illusion' of drinking water? What differentiates one illusion from another?

Are there different kinds of illusion? It doesn't help at all to keep perpetuating slogans without any reflection.

Reeti: I agree. For the longest time, I had no idea what it even meant to reflect on my experience. Did it mean how I felt, what I did, what I heard, or did it mean my deepest thoughts? I think that I was confusing reflection on experience with statements about feelings and emotions. For instance, in trying to describe my experience in specific situations, I would say things like "I was mad because so and so didn't treat me right"; or "I was jealous because so and so did better than me". Words like 'mad' and 'jealous', I slowly figured out, functioned as some kind of a label that actually hid my experience. It took me some time to see that such labels reduce experience to a fraction of what it is and using them makes the deeper experience inaccessible. These 'explanations' either justified my experience or even dismissed it by rationalizing it. After that all further reflection ceased. The only avenue left open was to adapt this cluster of concepts to myself just like everyone else.

Leela: It's a pity that we are so out of touch with our traditional ways of coping. Reflection on experience is the cornerstone of our traditions and we should try and make better use of this vast reservoir of knowledge. The Sanskrit word for experience, *anubhava*, suggests that it involves "an awareness of a state-of-being-in-the-world." *Anu* can be translated as apt or appropriate whereas *bhava* can be thought of as existence or being. So 'experience' means a way of being present in the world that is appropriate to whatever one encounters in the world. It is appropriate not in terms of a standard, but more in terms of being-present-with. Experience can be continually refined, and as we refine our ways of being-present-with, we can begin to think of experience in terms of a standard to be attained. To discover ways that are appropriate to the many different things we relate to in the world, we have to take time to get to know them. Proper experience involves something like a stance or a way of being we assume in the world with respect to our sensations, perception, feelings, and thoughts. We need to learn how to experience and think about experience. We need to modify it, channelize it, give form to it and fine-tune it in such a way that we have an appropriate way of being-in-the-world. Appropriate both in the subjective and objective sense of '*anu*' because our world is both objective and subjective at the same time, in the sense that it is 'our world' because it is also 'the world'.

Arya: Since there are layers upon layers of experience, can we say that it is not just *maya* alone that prevents access to our experience. Our culture, our society, and our individual psychologies are also impediments. Now it's easy to see how colonial consciousness creates extra barriers towards accessing experience, leaving almost a vacuum in its place.

Leela: This vacuum has been filled by the way we look at Indian culture and its texts – a way we learnt from the British. Our experiences are structured by language and by prior knowledge. By contrast, the way folks who are enlightened experience the natural world is not structured by language or prior knowledge. Instead, their experience is a relational attitude (*anu bhaava*). Among those of us who are not yet enlightened, experience is seen as a property of the experiencer or as that of the experienced. In this sense our experience is structured by language and prior knowledge.

Arya: Okay, I think we all agree that there is a world out there and that it has a pattern. So let's say that we pattern our world in different ways. This means that patterning is an activity undertaken by the person having the experience and this is because of *avidya* or *maya*. Now if we transcend *avidya* somehow, how can we know the pattern of the world?

Leela: Well, the fact that some patterns appear to work, and some work only for some time, and most not at all, suggests that the world is itself patterned, independent of the activity of the person having the experience. It could mean that the pattern of the world is compatible with multiple patterned activities. Or it could be something akin to providing multiple descriptions of human beings from different levels of observation, such as a genetic description, an anatomical description, a social description, and so on. We rightly believe that we describe the same reality, let's say, the human being. What is the nature of this reality? Does it consist of levels or aspects or dimensions or is the reality One? If the reality is One, how can multiple descriptions all be true? I have no answers to these philosophical problems, even though I do find them fascinating.

Reeti: So, if you and I both have this sense of 'I', can we distinguish between them?

Leela: Although in ordinary language-use the word 'I' signals the uniqueness of the person, in the *adhyatmic* context this is not the case. Here, the 'I' does not make us into individual persons but picks out something that is present in each entity capable of self-reference. We are different as bodies and as people, and can be distinguished as such. But we cannot be distinguished on the basis of the sense of 'I'. Through meditation we can go past our individual idiosyncrasies and experience the 'I' at the species level. When this happens we understand that this 'I' is neither our body nor our mind. Our bodies or our minds may become angry or feel sad, but the 'I' cannot be angry or sad. We think that it is our 'self' that is angry because we identify the 'I' with our individual selves. The enlightened describe the 'I' as a witness and tell us that identifying the individual with the *atman* or confusing the body with this 'I' is at the root of all our problems. At least this is what *Advaita* tells us. This has been elaborated in a number of different ways from the Jain 'I', to the *Dvaita* 'I', to the Buddhist 'non-I', and so on.

Arya: While I can understand a distinction between an experience and the cognitive scheme that structures it, I am having difficulty imagining a way of structuring experience that does not involve cognition.

Leela: Well, the enlightened tell us that their experience is not structured by cognition and they have devised many techniques to help us figure this out. For example, Zen Buddhism teaches us to stop cognitive activity in the process of understanding its koans. Many of the Indian traditions tell us that *dhyana* follows, and is different from, the phases that involve cognitive activities like seeing, hearing and understanding. Ultimately, we experience *gyaan udaya* or a dawning of knowledge. In this experience, there is a shattering of the sense of agency. It comes as a sort of a revelation, as though a veil is lifted from a person's eyes and they see the world for the first time. They realize that they were never an agent, even though they always thought they were one. They recognize this experience as such because they have heard of it as being a part of their tradition. They were seeking *ananda* and they find it in this knowledge, which is an experiential form of knowledge. Persons who have this experience realize that all their endeavors, projects, dreams, desires and frustrations were never really theirs. Their unhappiness arose not because they pursued these projects, but because they thought that they were theirs.

Reeti: But then whose projects were they? And from where did they have the experience of being an agent, or do such questions not make any sense?

Leela: Well, this insight into the nature of agency breaks radically with the experience of normal daily life. It tells us that our experience of daily life is something of an illusion and, by doing so, *reorganizes* the way our experience is structured. But this restructuring does not tell us how to go further, or what to do next. Enlightenment involves a restructuring of the traveled path, but says nothing about the path to traverse. Insofar as those who have had this experience still have a future, all they can do is act thoughtfully, and in this process try to sustain and develop their insight further. It means constantly attending to their insight in all their future endeavors.

Reeti: There are many well-documented stories of people who attain enlightenment at a very young age, as early as ten years old or even younger. Moreover, there are many who are completely illiterate, or those who don't follow any established practices and are nevertheless enlightened. This suggests that enlightenment is something that comes naturally to some people and is not necessarily a question of effort or study or reflection.

Leela: Unfortunately, this type of question cannot be answered scientifically any more than you can answer why Einstein came up with what he did. Our problem is not to try and figure out why some particular individual became enlightened, but how we can relate these individuals to our traditions, that is to say, to a learning process.

Arya: But people all over the world can become enlightened, even if they do not belong to any tradition, so why must it be related it to a tradition?

Leela: That may be true, but this does not further our understanding in any way. All we can do is acknowledge that people can get enlightened in many different ways. I am interested in studying enlightenment as a learning process. What someone learns is also learnable by another human being. That means to say it is also teachable. We had a plurality of teaching traditions that focused on teaching this to ordinary people. Therefore, if we want to study it scientifically, the more tractable question is: what are the strategies to become enlightened and how can they be taught? Individuals who are enlightened are interesting only insofar as they are confirmations that our traditions are still alive. But it is impossible to distinguish what is learnable and teachable in their process of becoming enlightened from what is unique to these particular individuals.

Reeti: In a way, this is the same as saying that not all human beings can become Olympic athletes or rocket scientists even though all of us can try to do so. It has to do with one's environment and traditions to a certain extent, but apart from that it is about natural disposition.

Leela: One's ability to become an athlete or a rocket scientist is conditional. It depends on one's biological inheritance, aptitude, schools, teachers, circumstances, and so on. Human happiness, according to how I understand the Indian traditions, is accessible to all. The fact, however, that all of us are not happy has led our traditions to investigate the things that stand in the way of human happiness. It has led them to discover various means and modalities to overcome these impediments. All human beings, if they seek happiness, can really become happy. 'Seek, and ye shall find', seems to be the message. Finding happiness is not a question of accident or luck; it is the guaranteed result of a search. As a consolation, our culture also tells us that we have an infinite number of births to accomplish this task. This story about rebirth alleviates the possibility of neurotic anxiety about wanting to find happiness.

Arya: I don't buy this story about rebirth. However, I can understand that such an attitude would have its advantages for those who believe in it. We've talked about agency and attachment to the idea of the self. But doesn't attachment basically refer to desires. How do we understand the idea that an enlightened person has no desires?

Leela: Before we understand what the idea says, it is good to be clear on what it does not say. Understanding this will allow us to appreciate yet another facet of our colonized minds. If you look at the way the Buddha is portrayed in text books, it appears as though he renounced all his desires. Yet if we read about the Buddha's road to enlightenment, we find something else: he did practice asceticism, but, he says, it did not help him to get enlightened! That is, even though some people do practice asceticism and can get enlightened because of it, this was not the Buddha's way. You find this sentiment echoed in the lives of many, many other enlightened people. They say that 'punishing their body' did not help them. So while it is indeed true that the Buddha said that desire is the root of sorrow, he did not say that one should therefore renounce desire. This popular interpretation of Buddhism has to do with who popularized Buddhism in the last few centuries, namely, the British, French and Germans. Two things are integral components of Christianity (in both the Protestant and Catholic versions): a deep suspicion of bodily cravings and a related asceticism. When the Europeans interpreted Buddhist thought, they did so through this prism and we have repeated their interpretation ever since. But if we realize that relating sorrow to desire is not merely Buddhist but also Upanishadic, we face a strange problem. There is no way to explain this, since renunciation was not an integral part of Vedic culture and the *Upanishads* do not neglect the fulfillment of desire, in fact they celebrate it. When human beings strive to find happiness, they want to find happiness *in their daily lives*. Consequently, a call to give up our daily lives that are replete with desire and to begin practicing asceticism cannot be the answer. Only those who teach us how to be happy in our ordinary day-to-day life have any chance of being heard.

Arya: I agree that it is not particularly helpful to oppose spirituality to desire or passion because one can pursue any passion such as fame, wealth, or power in a 'rational' way also. It's probably more about channeling one's abilities so that our actions can be brought under the scope of thoughtful consideration. What are some of the main insights that people have come up with relating to this?

Leela: Different traditions have different ways of describing their insights. The realization of the Buddhist traditions, for instance, is that to understand the illusory nature of agency requires an insight into the relation between the organism and its actions. I say 'traditions', because there are several ways of understanding the absence of agency even within these traditions. This is the principle of *anatta* they talk about. Or you could say that actions give rise to an illusory experience of agency.

The *Advaita* traditions have a different approach: They ask, "Who is 'she' who realizes that 'she' was never an agent? Whose illusion was it, and why did 'she' succumb to this illusion?" When these questions arise, the person discovers that there is a difference between 'her' persona and 'her' self. Here too different possibilities open up. Either the person discovers that the 'she' cannot be any 'particular she', because particularity is a property of the organism and the persona. Or they could experience the particularity of the 'she' in a different way than the particularity of the persona. In that case, you would be heading either towards the Jain traditions or towards the *Dvaita* traditions. Another realization could be that the illusion lies in the fact that you thought you were the agent, while you never really were. Actually, someone else is the agent and this agent acts through you all the time. You now see your role as a conduit and no more than that. In this, we approach the various *Bhakti* traditions.

Arya: Does belonging to a particular tradition have any bearing on the insight one gains? I guess I'm trying to figure out the extent to which Hindu enlightenment would be different from, say, Buddhist enlightenment or Sikh enlightenment.

Leela: Such a differentiation does not make sense. It is possible to differentiate between them only on the basis of the way in which they provide explanations for these experiential insights. For instance, a Buddhist might say that attachment to worldly things is at the root of the illusion that we are agents. If you contrast this with the way in which other Indian traditions explain the same insight you will see that it is not so much about doctrine but rather is more about the type of activity that each tradition emphasizes.

Reeti: I thought that the activities were pretty much the same in most of the Indian traditions. At the most they have different ways of chanting and meditating or different ways of dressing or different dietary codes.

Leela: Broadly speaking, that's true. But there are huge differences in the methodological approach between traditions and even within each tradition. For example, the path of *Gyana* or Knowledge tries to change the nature of experience by correcting it through unrelenting reflection and analysis. Who acts? What is acting? What is this attachment except the feeling of 'I' and 'mine'? What do these terms mean? Is the 'I' supposed to be this body, or this organism, or this persona? Does the sense of 'I' undergo change and development as the organism or the persona undergoes change and development? If not, what is the relation between the 'I' and the other two things?

Another way of reaching the same insight is to go even deeper into experience. Any attachment requires constancy of the object or the event that one is attached to, and of the 'agent' who is attached. The deeper one delves into locating this constancy in experience, the more one discovers discontinuities. One discovers that neither the structures of experience nor their constancy are given in experience. Rather, they are provided by the descriptions of the experience. This would be the path of *Dhyana* or Meditation. By relocating the subordinate units of daily experience, the meditative path restructures it.

Another way of achieving the same insight is to notice that attachment is also a particular human emotion. To be unattached requires an altering of this emotion. This can be done by using other kinds of human emotions as meta-emotions directed towards emotional attachment. Ironical and humorous descriptions of situations enable the person to achieve a sense of distance from this attachment; music, rhythm, dance and poetry also work to generate such sets of meta-emotions. Or compassion directed towards suffering caused by attachment will help loosen the hold of the attachment. This is the path of *Bhakti* or Devotion that helps lead to such an insight. This path restructures experience by altering the force of emotions invested in such experiences.

Or one could arrive at the same insight by trying to sever the relation between action and its outcome. Here attachment is seen as the experience of relating action to its outcome. A seeker decouples action from intention by building a sort of reflexivity regarding action and 'its' intention. One acts observantly – observing both the nature of action and 'its' alleged intention, to discover that intentionality is no property of the 'agent' at all. This is the path of *Karma* or Action. This path transforms daily experience by severing the relation between human action and human intentionality.

Yet another way to approach this insight is to realize that no matter what one experiences, there is but one means through which one can experience, that is through one's body. So one can begin to understand what experience is by experimenting with the experience itself. One's body is not only the means through which experience is possible but it is also the instrument to experiment on experience itself. Thus, the focus shifts to the body and its sense organs. These are the various paths of *Yoga* and *Tantra* that help in furthering this insight.

Reeti: But as far as I can tell, each of the indigenous Indian traditions uses most of these activities and paths. This means it would be difficult to differentiate between traditions on these terms.

Leela: That's right. The suggestion that 'Buddhism' and 'Hinduism' are two different traditions is a claim about one's classificatory scheme and is not a claim about the structure of the world. It is not based on 'doctrinal' differences. The examples I just gave are based on one single insight about attachment. Naturally, with a shift in emphasis on other things and with various permutations and combinations this division sometimes makes no sense at all or at other times becomes even starker. Even when we speak in terms of activities, it is obvious that each is present in the other: reflection on experience cannot be undertaken without emotion; poetry and music without thought are impossible; one cannot go deeper into experience without thinking about experience; reflexivity without thought and emotion is impossible. This captures the diversity within the Indian traditions and can account not only for the disputes but also for the similarities among these different traditions.

Arya: So the real question to figure out in such contexts would be: what is the domain of disputes between say, a Shankara and a Buddha, or between the *naastikas* and the *aastikas*?

Leela: Indeed. Is it philosophical anthropology, or human psychology, or what? This is an interesting question for further research. Nevertheless, such disputes can be very productive. They can prevent dogmatism and generate new methods through cross-fertilization of techniques and strategies. This is both necessary and desirable. No particular teaching process can teach every individual in the same way and to the same extent. The presence of a multiplicity of teaching methods can only increase their total efficacy.

Arya: As I understand it, the path of *Gyana* along with the teachings contained in the *Upanishads* seems to be the highest path. Would you say that the kind of knowledge that can be derived from stories in the *Puranas* is a simplified version of these same teachings because not everyone is capable of meditating or studying the *Upanishads*?

Leela: Not at all. This would mean that enlightenment consists of a vertical hierarchy of knowledge elements and that one can become enlightened only after going through the elementary, secondary and graduating steps. If this is what you want to argue, then you will be committed to saying that there is only one route to enlightenment. This makes enlightenment conditional upon possessing some specific ability. In the same way that not every undergraduate student in physics can go on to do research in physics, this would mean that only some people can attain enlightenment. The truth is that in India followers of *all* paths think that their path is the best way to enlightenment. Being happy or enlightened (as you know, I use these two words as synonyms) is like doing research in physics. It is not an 'end state'; it is a goal only in the sense that 'doing research in physics' can be a goal. Whether you do research in plasma physics or solid state physics, you are doing research in physics. In the same way, the *Upanishads* and the *Puranas* both help you find happiness. There is no hierarchy of any sort between them, or any other path. If you do not consider doing simple *puja* and learning from *Puranic* stories as a way to achieve enlightenment and claim that only *gyana* leads one to enlightenment, then you will not be able to account for the fact that many illiterate people, with their simple practice of doing a daily *puja*, with no knowledge of the *Upanishads*, also achieve enlightenment. In fact, there are many more such people than those who became enlightened by studying the *Upanishads* or any other text.

Arya: Well, it's just that I know that the *Puranic* stories are not meant to be descriptions of the world, whereas I do take the statements in the *Upanishads* to be descriptions of the world and therefore consider them to be at a sort of a higher level. As you pointed out, the Buddhist insight about desire being at the root of sorrow is as much *Upanishadic* as it is Buddhist. In fact it is an experiential insight not confined to any specific tradition. Does this not mean that such insights are supposed to be descriptions of the world, and labels such as Buddhist or *Advaitic* simply identify the origin of these theories? Sort of like how Einstein's theory of relativity tells us that he formulated it in the first place.

Leela: Not quite. These insights are primarily guides to action that are rooted in experience and help you in transforming experience. Even though such insights have a descriptive role, they are not descriptions of the world.

Arya: But this does not make much sense. What are they describing if not the world?

Leela: I think it would help to think of them as being analogous to route descriptions. A route description would instruct you to make a left or a right or to carry on straight and it would provide you with landmarks to make sure you're on the right track. In this sense, these insights are not doctrines or even straightforward descriptions of the world. They are 'route descriptions' relativized both to the route and to the individual on that route. It always depends on the stage of moral and spiritual development of the individual and their efficacy is always relative to the experience, context, and inclinations of the individual in question. Because of this, it is not possible to speak either about the truth or about the falsity of such traditions but only about whether or not some route description is successful in teaching an individual to go about in the world experimentally. The insights of the Indian traditions are guides for orienting ourselves in unfamiliar territory. This unfamiliar territory, of course, refers to our individual experience.

Reeti: That's odd considering that we have a certainty about our experience and our emotional states that goes far beyond any other kind of certainty we can imagine.

Leela: On the surface it does seem like that. We have the conscious ability to distinguish various emotions from one another. How do we know that we are angry? How do we know that we are not confusing happiness with anger? The very absurdity of these questions tells us that we are speaking of an entirely different kind of certainty. Not only that, it indicates that the ability to know that we are angry and not happy has something to do with the structure of these emotions. And yet, we are unable to say what this alleged structure is. For instance, imagine someone in a terrible state of jealousy. Then they happen to discover that their jealousy was totally misplaced, and all of a sudden, like flipping a switch, their emotional state changes from jealousy to relief. But what exactly happens? What is the structural shift that suddenly occurs? We have no idea. Our emotional worlds may be obvious to each one of us; but familiar, they certainly are not. That is why we need guidance navigating in this world.

Reeti: And how exactly do these 'route maps' function to help us orient ourselves?

Leela: Imagine you're on a journey and there's a destination you want to reach. The destination is not specified, but there are many different ways to get there. Each of these route descriptions assures us that it will bring us to the destination and there are no time limits to arrive there either. Now, we have very little to go by, so how do we judge which route description to pick? In the first place, this depends on the individual. What sense of ease or urgency they have, how fast they want to travel, or how much they want to enjoy the scenery. To the extent that we are already on a path, we choose a route description that is best able to describe what we have already seen or what we are currently seeing. Besides, our experiences are shaped by the tradition we are born into; therefore there is an inclination to look at our own traditions first. Only when such a search fails do we cast around for other route descriptions which are closer to our experience. The route description should make sense to the individual and it can do so only if it is a true description of their individual experiences. It is this that relativizes the route description to the individual and to the route they are on. Like all such descriptions it tells us where to go, how to get there, and identifies what we might see along the way. Therefore, we can say that the role that the route description plays as a description of the world is subordinated to its ability to guide us on that route. Its description is true only for that route and it is true only insofar as you are on that route and not on another.

Arya: Couldn't we say the same for all 'route descriptions' including those provided by religion?

Leela: Actually there is a big difference. Route descriptions provided by religion claim that only one of the routes will take you to the golden palace, which, they specify, is your destination. All other descriptions will lead you straight to the camp of the cannibals. Thus, we are provided with 'objective' criteria for choosing between competing route descriptions. These descriptions specify the nature of the territory, the goal of the journey, provide a complete description of the route, and tell you what happens if you are on the wrong route. Not just that. They specify that there is a time limit for you to reach your destination, that is, before you die. In this case the criterion of 'efficiency' cannot be relativized to individual 'ease' any more, but becomes very objective instead. Religions are such route descriptions. They too are guides to action but not in the way that the Indian traditions are.

Another big difference is that just because a route description makes sense of the past and current experiences of an individual, it does not mean that it will always continue to do so. The Indian traditions encourage you to proceed thoughtfully on your journey and continually question what you see. In other words, these route descriptions inculcate the ability to go about in the world *experimentally*.

Arya: Well, if we're talking about personal predilections, then why is it that some people choose absurdly difficult paths? There are some *sadhus* who take strict celibacy vows, so much so that they're never supposed to set eyes on women, including their own mothers; and women are not allowed into temples when they are around. I think that this is an awfully discriminatory attitude towards women. As if even seeing a woman is a sexual crime that will upset their spiritual balance! I think this is utter rubbish.

Leela: I don't think this is rubbish at all, but for the sake of argument let's grant that the vow of celibacy is indeed rubbish. You cannot, however, deny them the freedom to believe in this 'rubbish' and practice it for themselves. There is nothing morally wrong in having wrong or false beliefs. Atheists, for instance, genuinely believe that religion is very dangerous for human beings but that does not mean, therefore, that people should be forbidden from being believers. The non-celibate men and women who follow the same sects as these *sadhus* share these customs and do not protest that they are not allowed to enter the temples when the *sadhus* are present. They do not feel discriminated against. The reason you feel this way lies in the normative assumptions you make and not in the beliefs of the *sadhus*. It may be more productive to question your own normative beliefs rather than the beliefs of the *sadhus*. If you agree that there are many different paths to happiness, you cannot rule out paths that don't make sense to you. I have known some great men who practiced very strict *Brahmacharya* because they were *bhaktas* of Hanuman, himself a very strict *Brahmachari*. This is as legitimate a way of being in the world as any other and I am not sympathetic to looking at it as some kind of a deviation. Such people are present in all cultures, so we have to assume that this is a variety in human evolution, and our traditions recognize the need for celibacy as something that some people might opt for.

Reeti: I agree that it's not fair to suggest that any of the extreme paths are abnormal in any way, even though it is hard to relate to fringe lifestyles.

Leela: I think the problem arises when we thoughtlessly take over 'route descriptions' that have no relevance to us. We must develop novel ways of understanding cultural diversity. People have hardly reflected on what kinds of diversity exist or on appropriate ways of describing it. We have catalogued cultural diversity but have failed to understand what we describe. Diversity does not merely mean that there are different traditions, but that they are different in different ways.

Arya: What I fail to understand is why our sages did not write proper 'how-to' manuals. Also, even though there are many enlightened people, they themselves do not seem capable of properly theorizing about their experience.

Leela: Well, reflection on experience was itself taught experientially because the results of such reflection (which transform experience) can only be experiential. But many of them did write practical 'manuals' and we have a vast body of literature to show for it. The problem is that we have lost the ability to make sense of this body of work. The transmission of these abilities is a part of the transmission of the theories. That is why reading the *Gita* (or any other text) is of little use on its own. The Guru, I think, is indispensable to the transmission process; because they would tell us *how* to read these texts

as instructions for action. We have theories in the form
of the books of Shankara or Abhinavagupta, or numerous other sages, but we have difficulty in doing much
with them other than writing 'learned' tracts. As Indians, if we have to access our traditions we must know
how to access them *the Indian way*. Currently, we access the Indian traditions the way the West has taught us
to access them – as texts. So it's not as if we have lost
some 'textual interpretative tradition.' If that was all
there was to it, the existing set of Sanskrit pundits could
solve the problem. In fact, the Sanskrit pundits have
transformed the problem of understanding Indian texts
into a problem of interpretation as well. Now we need
to reinvent the Indian way of going about with these
texts, through the language of the present, and driven by
our contemporary exigencies.

Reeti: But in any case most Indians do not turn to books for
help. In times of crisis or when we need to cope with
unhappiness, most likely we will resort to chanting or
other rituals rather than any sort of intellectual reflection. We rely on the knowledge gleaned from our stories
and proverbs and at the most we learn a mantra or two.
So I wonder how relevant it is to talk about the lack of
understanding of our texts.

Leela: I think it would help to take a broad view on this. Our
traditions make the claim that every human being can be
happy. Any and all ways are conducive to reaching this
end-state: thinking, meditation, music, dance, sex, celibacy, and yes, even going to temples. At any and every
stage, people can achieve happiness. Such a structure of
society is the most ideal 'social security system' that can
ever be built. The system guarantees each one of us that
we can be happy and provides us with just the route we
can follow to become happy. Like all social security systems, this one also needs to be constantly replenished. It
too has to draw upon the total wealth of society to keep

it going. This wealth must also be continually reproduced: new stories, new rituals, and new performances
of what already exists, drama, poetry, and so on. For this
to happen, people must continue to see what is being
produced as 'wealth'.

What happens when slowly, over a period of time, people do not see it as wealth anymore? The system slowly
starts unraveling because new contributions to this 'social security system' are not seen as contributions to
such a system any more. This does not mean that people
all of a sudden change their ways of looking at things.
Some still see stories as wealth, that is to say, they can
learn from them; some still go to *hari katha*, and learn
from it; some still go to the temples and find happiness
in the *puja*. But the 'social security system' slowly starts
falling apart. It cannot be sustained and ceases to be the
safety net that it once was to all the people. But it does
not completely disappear or totally disintegrate because
it is in the nature of this society to build such a net. So,
even as parts begin to become unsustainable, there are
new attempts to rejuvenate the entire system. Our colonial consciousness is about one aspect of the how and
the why of this unraveling. We see that many have opted
out of the system. But it is my conviction that 'private
insurance' will never work. It can never provide us with
the safety net that was to be found in the time honored
traditions that our culture had to offer.

Reeti: That's a great pity. The only silver lining is that we are
at least gradually becoming aware of our problems.
There's a lot that we need to unravel and decipher, but
there's much that we can still relate to. We still have an
intuitive understanding of our traditions so we can try
and work out ways to salvage the situation.

Leela: I'm afraid, here's where we need to confront something
really disturbing. We no longer have an intuitive understanding of many of the concepts or words and meanings, especially when it comes to talking about human

psychology. We are as clueless about these words as anyone from the West or any other culture who wants to study our traditions.

Reeti: I'll be the first to admit that I speak only in English when talking about anything serious. But I feel like I do have an intuitive understanding of words such as *ahamkara, chitta, manas, bhavana,* and their kin.

Leela: Actually, I think we pretty much do the same thing with these words as we do with the other words we talked about like *deva* and *puja.* We map them on to certain words in English and understand them in the way that the West has taught us to understand them. Ask yourself the following questions: Is there a difference between *mano bhavana* and *mano vikara*? Is *chitta shuddhi* the same as not having any *mano vikara*? If yes, *chitta* and *manas* refer to the same entity; if no, what is the difference? It is my claim that we are as clueless as anyone from the West who studies these things. What they learn from studying Patanjali is also what we learn by studying Patanjali. Actually, the cards are stacked in their favor because their understanding of their native language (say, English) is more profound than our understanding of English. In our case, we are deceived because we can use these words proficiently (albeit unreflectively); we believe that we know what these words mean and what they refer to. We do not. We have taken to English the way ducks take to water because we no longer intuitively know what words from our own languages mean! This is the reason why earlier generations of Indians did not object to the translations the British came up with. It's because our understanding of *Ishwara* is as shallow as our understanding of God.

Arya: But only a very small percentage of Indians speak English. At the time the British came up with their translations, this percentage would have been miniscule.

Leela: The problem is not confined just to translation into English. The way we talk in our native Indian languages har-
bors the exact same problem. The framework of the
western cultural experience has been so dominant in the
last 300 years that language-use in Hindi, Kannada,
Tamil, Gujarati, Marathi, Sanskrit, and every other Indian language has been distorted. A first distortion of
the Indian traditions took place when the missionaries
and scholars started translating them. (Naturally, distortions had already begun under Islamic colonization, but
let's try and keep this picture manageable.) A second
distortion took place when Indians themselves adopted
this way of talking in English. A third distortion occurred when Indians then translated this way of talking
in English back into the Indian languages. After all these
distortions, there is no way of finding out what the original usage of these words was. We also do not know how
the cognition of Indians has changed after these various
stages of distortion.

Reeti: I don't mean to downplay our predicament, but isn't it
also the case that we have to be enlightened before we
can fully understand some words such as *atman* and
chitta? Besides, Indians don't really discuss their feelings and emotions the way Americans do, so how significant is this, really?

Leela: But these words have to do with basic human psychology! We cannot do without words to think about ourselves, our friends, husbands, wives, parents, kids, and
other human beings. Given the fundamental importance
of a vocabulary that allows us to talk about ourselves,
we cannot sit back and rely on a community of specialists who can anyway only explain what a Patanjali or a
Shankara meant. Even if they tell us what these words
mean, how do we understand them in ourselves? Is my
desire for a *dosa* an expression of my *manas* or my *buddhi*? When I want to punch somebody, what prevents
me: *buddhi, chitta, manas, dharma*, or, to use Christian

terminology, the conscience? What if my *buddhi* and *manas* both support me in wanting to punch someone? What then is the difference between the two? What do I need to train if I want to improve? How do I identify that entity? How do I know what trains it? Your experts, it turns out, will have to appeal to the words I already know in order to explain to me what *buddhi* or *manas* is. Merely knowing a word cannot help me identify it in myself. Finally, it is not a mere loss of words that is at stake: it is about the accessibility or non-accessibility of our daily experience and our ability to think about it. We do not talk much about emotions, you say. Perhaps it is true. But that is not an explanation as to why concepts from human psychology do not make sense to us anymore. We need to look for an explanation of this state of affairs elsewhere. That is what I am trying to do.

Arya: I guess it's because we no longer have the institutional structures and intellectual engagement that constantly reworked and refined the meanings of our technical terms. Even the topics of debate and the manner in which we debate has changed.

Leela: It's worse than you can imagine. Our new debates – our academic social science debates, our popular 'intellectual' debates – appear to exist completely disembodied from and irrelevant to the reality of our lives. Now we need to start the process of reflecting on our cultural experience, and refashion terms as they are relevant to our needs. We should reach into the past only to identify whether their problems were similar to ours, and whether they came up with answers that can still make sense to us in the twenty-first century.

Reeti: I feel certain that many of the psychological insights generated by our ancestors are still relevant to us today. I was hoping we would end on a more optimistic note now that we're coming to the end of our brief sojourn together. I hope we can still come up with some constructive ideas to make amends.

CHAPTER IX

TOWARDS A CULTURAL RENAISSANCE

Reeti: It occurred to me that for those of us who live in the West, the problems we just discussed must be that much more compounded. Don't you think so?

Leela: Of course. Hindus living outside India do not have the luxury of living in an environment where the transmission of their traditions takes place organically. They often find themselves in situations where they have to explain their traditions to others as well as to their own kids. They then begin to lament the fact that their parents did not teach them anything about Hinduism so they have nothing to pass along to their kids. They don't realize that their knowledge or ignorance relating to Hinduism is exactly the same as the knowledge or ignorance of ordinary Hindus living in India. Had they remained in India, their lack of knowledge would not have worried them. They would have been able to transmit their traditions on to their kids in the same way as millions do in India – without any explicit instruction in the 'religion' called Hinduism. But in America or elsewhere in the world, our social and cultural environment forces us to articulate our understanding of our traditions in a particular way, based on the religious framework of Christianity. In western culture it makes sense to ask certain questions. We start fabricating all sorts of responses to these questions as if such questions are perfectly intelligible to us. It does not occur to Indians that instead of trying to answer questions that we don't relate to, we should try and understand the culture that generates these types of questions.

Arya: It took all of five days, but your point has finally sunk in. Seriously, we should have been provoked into studying this entity called religion a long time ago. Instead of doing that, we've been busy trying to construct a 'Hinduism' to fit into the image of religion.

Leela: Hindus don't realize that by trying to codify our vast array of stories, we are transforming the Hindu traditions into a rigid body of canonical scriptures. Since we now consider them to be scriptures, we will no longer be able to retell our stories in a myriad different ways. The stories will be treated as sacred doctrines that need to be protected. Needless to say, our Hindu brethren have jumped on this bandwagon as well and are ever-ready to protect our 'sacred' texts. This is ignorant on so many levels. Just because they treat it like a religion, does not mean that a Hindu religion has come into being. The problem remains that even though Hindus have adopted words like 'religion' they do not know what these words mean and the extent to which semantic and experiential distortion takes place in the process of adopting these words.

Reeti: If we consider the ease with which most Indians, including the hard-core Hindu nationalists, concede that Hinduism is not really a religion, it's quite clear that the term 'religion' does not mean much to them. But in their defense, I will say that some of their protests are justified. As we are well aware, American universities have been churning out legions of scholars who go about masquerading as experts on Hinduism, spreading their rubbish that is often quite mean-spirited. In fact, one renowned American scholar of Hinduism described the *Gita* as a book that promotes war and violence. In an article for an encyclopedia, no less! I think that there does need to be some sort of Hindu representation that can challenge such people and prevent such thoughtless negative portrayals. I am also concerned as a parent because I don't want my kids being embarrassed or ashamed when they read such descriptions. Besides, I don't want Americans reading such articles to think of Hinduism as weird and different.

Leela: Yes, I do remember the furor over the encyclopedia article on the *Gita*. But then, what happened next? One of our fellow Hindus stepped in to replace that article, except what they ended up doing was merely repeating the same old colonial story about Hinduism, only without the derogatory remarks. The question you need to consider is this: Is this effective in the achievement of your goal? It most certainly is not. By trying to make Hinduism an acceptable religion that does not seem weird to Americans, the Indian community reproduces the western colonial endeavor of making Hindu culture into a variant of Christianity. And what is the result? Americans think Hinduism is just like Christianity, but a bit dark and ridiculous since it needs all these strange deities in order to worship God. So by trying to show that Hinduism is not weird and different, you end up affirming that it is similar but inferior. This is not an effective way to solve the problems of the Hindu community. Such efforts are bound to fail because the negativity is located in the framework itself – a framework that is now shared by the Hindu community.

Arya: Why do you say that the framework itself is negative?

Leela: It forces us to live according to the standard set by a 'rational', 'spiritual' and 'true' religion such as Christianity. In order to do so, we have to accept its criteria of what counts as cogent arguments and good reasons in the realm of religion. Conversely, we are forced to see certain things as superstition, or meaningless ritual, or to see our gods as immoral.

Reeti: It's depressing, but I feel like it is impossible to get out of the current dominant framework.

Leela: We have no choice. As long as we merely agree to settle for a benign portrayal of our traditions rather than developing an alternative framework, our efforts are bound to fail. Your sons and daughters will inherit the shame and embarrassment about their culture that are intrinsic to this way of looking at things. Right now we are merely following the footsteps of our colonial masters and the missionaries. We have succumbed to evangelical propaganda and colonial education. The result is this massive attempt to transform our various indigenous traditions into a 'Hindu religion', which is basically a form of Protestant theology dressed up in Hindu garb. If we fight our battles at this level, the outcome is predictable. The entire struggle will take place within the intellectual constraints set by American society and its academics. In the end, American Hindus will truly complete the work of the missionaries: we will have converted ourselves into Protestant Christians. This is what the Brahmo Samaj, the Arya Samaj and their progeny have done in India. Just as these organizations have developed a sanitized version of 'Hinduism' that lives up to the Christian model of a religion with a rational foundation, this is what the various Hindu foundations in America will do if they continue along the same lines.

Arya: If I wasn't all too familiar with Hindu buffoonery, I would suspect that what is happening today is part of some planned missionary strategy. I was appalled at what the various Hindu foundations in America were suggesting as material for textbooks on Hinduism. Wherever the textbooks mentioned Hindu stories or 'writings', they wanted to replace it with Hindu 'scriptures'; where the textbooks discuss enlightenment, these foundations wanted it replaced with 'God realization'. 'Brahman' was systematically replaced by 'God'. And even worse, they wanted to deny that the Hindu traditions revolve around multiple 'gods'. They insisted that all of these different deities are in fact one God, or at the most various forms of God. No wonder their case was thrown out by the judge.

Leela: This is exactly what I mean! With these proposals they are basically trying to make the Christian conceptualization of God into the main focus of Hinduism. By contrast, in India we can conceptualize 'God' in a myriad different ways. We can select Ganesha as our *ishta devata* (chosen deity), without acknowledging any one God whom he is supposed to embody. We can strive for *adhyatmic* knowledge and totally deny the existence of God. We can live in complete ignorance of the Hindu 'scriptures' and still be Hindu. According to the image that the various Hindu foundations want to promote, such Hindus, that is to say the majority of the Hindu population, are ignorant of true 'Hinduism', its 'scriptures' and its 'God'. Basically, these foundations are neither continuing the traditions as passed on by our ancestors, nor critically reflecting upon them.

Arya: Well, most Hindus are oblivious of the scope and depth of the problem. The way we carry on makes it seem like all our problems merely revolve around some derogatory remarks and negative portrayals. As if we will have solved anything by leaving out some sexually explicit paragraphs or banning some silly books!

Leela: To be fair, I think that the matter may be a bit more complex. We're overlooking another dynamic that forces us to stay within the existing framework. American identity politics seems to force each minority community to assert itself as a separate 'church' with its own distinct religious or ethnic identity. Identity politics seems to be the way in which the dominant culture in America compels other cultural communities to become variants of itself. This is what seems to have happened with all communities that struggled for recognition, such as the Irish Catholics, Jews, blacks, or even the gay and feminist movements. They can invoke the strategies of the human rights discourse and can assert the value of their culture within certain limits. Their cultural identity is accepted only when it takes on a recognizable, non-threatening form, that is, once it ceases to be a true alternative to the dominant culture. I can easily see the Hindu community becoming the next church-like ghetto culture.

Reeti: With the way we're headed, this mission will soon be accomplished by the various Hindu foundations of America. Sooner or later they will complete the task of transforming our traditions into a Hindu-Protestant church. These Hindu foundations are more harmful to our traditions than all of the missionaries and Indologists of this world.

Leela: We should pay attention to this because what is happening in America and Europe in terms of Hinduism may well portend the shape of things to come in India a few decades from now. We would do well to learn from these mistakes. A deeper insight into colonial consciousness is of far greater value than a continuing requiem on the greatness of the Indian past, which is what many of these cultural organizations tend to propagate. Such a consciousness is characterized by a double impotency. It is impotent to access its own cultural experience and it is equally impotent to access the experience of western culture. This type of impotent consciousness constitutes the class of Indian intellectuals today, both in India and abroad. Is there any wonder that they fail to produce any interesting reflections on either political or cultural theory? Is there any wonder they are incapable of bringing about a regeneration of Indian culture?

Reeti: That's so true. That is why it has been such a pleasure listening to your ideas. They promise to open up many different avenues of research and compel us to take a fresh approach. Our agenda for the future, then, seems to be clear. Now we should take up these same domains of study and try to describe how there are different ways of going about in the world.

Leela: Bear in mind that the problem is not merely about representing another way of going about in the world. There is a deeper issue involved. Whenever we study another culture, we have this compelling intuition that different cultures have a different conception of religion, or morality, or self, or whatever. Although we notice differences, we believe that it is merely a different conception of the same domain. However, it is not at all obvious that we (from two different cultures) are talking about the same domain. If we were to put the descriptions of the moral domain next to each other, it is impossible to avoid the equally compelling conclusion that they could not possibly belong to the same domain. These culture-specific conceptions are only appropriate at different levels of description. These are the kinds of problems we need to unravel. Are we even talking about the same domain of study when we talk about religion and ethics and psychology or are we talking about completely different things? I have approached these problems by taking a unique entry point. I look at the western descriptions of India and see them as expressions of western culture itself. Once the conceptual limitations of their approach are identified, it becomes possible to focus our energies on developing alternative descriptions. In this way, the rich storehouse of knowledge embodied by the Indian traditions can be rediscovered and translated into the conceptual language of the present times.

Reeti: Could it be that it is already too late? Have we, psychologically speaking, already become a variant of the western psyche?

Leela: I think that this possibility is unlikely. Colonial rule did not destroy Indian culture; it merely modified it in some way. If cultures are configurations of learning, and this particular configuration of learning was not destroyed, then what we see in Indian culture today is an adaptation of some of its learning processes. (This is my assumption.) The psychology of the members of any particular culture is formed by the coordination of many social and cultural structures. These range from patterns of family interactions, through educational institutions, to peer group interactions. Even if each of these were modified under colonial rule, it involved a modification and not their destruction. Consequently, there is a distinction between colonial consciousness and Indian cultural psychology. We have learnt to get by with our colonial consciousness; we notice its presence only vaguely and dimly; but this consciousness is not (yet) a part of the cultural psychology of Indians. We do not need to find an 'original' or 'uncorrupted' Indian cultural psychology to make this suggestion. It is sufficient to suggest that a cultural psychology in a culture is formed by different processes and structures and that most of them were not destroyed under colonial rule.

Arya: Actually, this is not just about our cultural psychology, but also involves institutional structures and political theory.

Leela: Well, the civilizing mission (or educational project) of colonialism was an attempt to create the conditions of intelligibility for Christian conceptual schemes among the Indian population. Here the role of institutional structures such as the state, law, courts, and schools was very important. It's not as if the assumptions of western-Christian thought somehow spread magically among the Indians. We can try and trace the process by which the colonial institutional structures compelled Indians to adopt certain attitudes which functioned as the conditions of intelligibility for western-Christian conceptual schemes. This process was never fully successful, the conditions of intelligibility were never fully realized, but the attitudes created by colonialism among certain layers of the Indian population went a long way towards making them behave as though these conceptual schemes made perfect sense to them.

Reeti: Okay, so we can begin by trying to decolonize the social sciences and go on to trace the spread of colonial ideas in Indian society. Then what would the next steps be?

Leela: The nature of Indian culture was simply this: the knowledge that it produced was a means to reflect upon and form experience. It is the transmission of this that has been arrested. Our task is to take up anew the challenge our culture posed and answered so successfully in the past: reflect on human experience and relate these reflections to our experience so that it can be molded, changed, formed and transformed. It's now up to us to pick up the pieces. We are students of science and we know that the sciences are one of the best examples of human knowledge. First of all, we need to distinguish between science and pseudo-science. We can then confront the following task: how to reestablish our connection to the Indian traditions, *including its way of teaching* to reflect on human experience. There is no direct way to do so. Out of sheer necessity we have to go through the prism of scientific theorizing. We need to develop ways of thinking about experience in a systematic fashion, and science, in the first place, is systematic thinking. This means that we have to bring together two threads in human history which developed completely independent of each other: the practical way of teaching and thinking about human experience and a theoretical way of reflecting about nature. Our road to the former is through the latter. To put it a bit absurdly: we must teach practically in a scientific way or build scientific theories in a practical way.

Reeti: Do you have any idea, or can you think of any examples of what success in this endeavor would look like?

Leela: Keep in mind that scientific progress does not mean that we will be able to come up with a set of notes that 'explains everything'. We have to first try to formulate the problem properly; we have to try and build some kind of a hypothesis that might solve the problem; we have to test our hypotheses, and so on. If we could come up with a scientific theory that answers questions about at least some aspects relating to our culture, it would be a good start. I would like to know the following: what were the Indian thinkers of antiquity busy with? What problems did they try to solve and what were their solutions? Are their problems even relevant to us in the twenty-first century? If yes, how can we reformulate them so that they become susceptible to scientific enquiry? Is it possible to endorse their problems and their solutions without buying into some of their other claims (about previous births and karma, for instance)? In short, did the Indians produce any knowledge in the course of the millennia? If yes, what kind of knowledge is it and can we express it in modern language? Answers to some of these questions would be an example of success.

Reeti: I just want to say that this has been one of the most satisfying holidays I've ever had. I'm very glad that you took the time to tell us about what you've been busy working on over the past couple of decades. Although what you say makes a lot of intuitive sense to me, I still want to ask, how can we be certain that you have a true understanding of the situation or whether you merely think that you are right? How can we be sure that it is not merely your personal prejudices against the West or your own conceptual limitations as an Indian that you've bundled together as an 'explanation'?

Leela: There are a number of ways to test theories, from checking them against our own experiences to drawing conclusions from arguments. That is what knowledge and objectivity is all about. Am I ranting and raving, or am

I saying something worth thinking about and exploring further? I am not trying to compare our culture with western culture to say that one is better than the other. Nor am I am interested in embarking on a condemnation or moral judgment of either the East or the West. What I want to do is to try and understand both. I am committed to a scientific understanding of cultures, and science, as we all know, is very much a product of western culture, so how can I be prejudiced against the West? My criticisms of the West revolve around one point only: Has it produced knowledge or does it talk rubbish when it talks about other cultures?

Arya: I have one more question. Are our efforts towards a revitalization of the Indian traditions going to be primarily an intellectual endeavor or is this something that will be spread across wide layers of society?

Leela: What intellectuals say percolates down in a hundred different ways into the daily lives of all types of people. Intellectual insights are reformulated in many different ways by different people. Music, dance, poetry, film, *hari katha, yakshagana*, and other regional forms of expression rework these insights in their own ways as well. However, this must be a continuous process because the world we live in changes all the time. Insights must be redeveloped, retold and recast in new idioms, and ever newer ways of reformulating them must be developed. So it's most certainly not just a small group of people called intellectuals or university professors that can do this. Anyone who reflects on life is an intellectual. Colonialism affected this process of reflection drastically. Our insights are frozen at many different levels. This does not mean that nobody in India understands them. But what should have been a continuous process of interaction has now frozen at multiple levels.

Reeti: I'm beginning to see a ray of hope. Something tells me that the tide will turn and we will be able to bring about a cultural regeneration to reconnect meaningfully to our traditions.

Leela: I'm reminded of this verse from the Gita that most of us are familiar with that says: "whenever *dharma* begins to wane and *adharma* waxes, to protect the good and punish the wicked, and to re-establish *dharma*, I fashion myself." You also know how most of us have been taught to understand these verses: Krishna's *avatar* always comes around to set things right and that this will happen again and again. However, when I read this with my current sensibilities, here is what I find striking. These verses could be telling us the following: There is a process of learning to be *dharmic* and this is a natural learning process in society. It is inevitable that any social learning process can and does undergo degeneration. When such degeneration occurs, at some critical phase, other mechanisms in society will kick in and regenerate the process by which we can once again learn to be *dharmic*. Of course, the writers of the *Gita* formulate this insight using the imagery familiar to them: Krishna and his *avatars* fighting against the wicked and promoting the good. But that need not deter us. What we need to consider is their insight into the nature of society. How did they discover these things? How did they discuss these things? What kind of research did they do? If indeed Indian civilization produced any knowledge, we must be able to state what it is using twenty-first century language. Today the results of my research can become the starting points for the next generation of researchers. On this, I pin my hopes. In the meantime, all I can do is keep on truckin', bearing in mind that *karmanye vadhikaraste* . . . .